Kim Alexander

The Path that led me to the Cover

The strength within an empath that overpowers a narcissist

contents

introduction	1
the dark night of the soul	5
spiritual awakening	15
the golden mask	23
how to spot a narcissist	45
the super empath	59
boundaries	69
the super empath and the narcissist	79
healing	89
your intuition is your biggest gift	103
the power of not giving a fuck	115
never judge unless you've walked someone's path	127
health	133
pink rock	155
my purpose and my vision	161
the people I need to thank	166
one year later ...	167

Narcissists and super empaths (over sensitive) seem to be a big topic of conversation these days, but why and how is it happening? If an empath is soft and a narcissist is dark, why are the two drawn to each other? What is the attraction and how can we stop this attraction from growing?

My story digs deep into my past and unravels the whys and how? Better still, it tells you what not to do, so you can avoid getting involved with a narcissist.

I was reflecting on my inner demons and past traumas. I needed to heal myself and let go of them. Once we understand how we can do this and who we are as a person, not what our trauma is, we CAN heal by using strong boundaries, following our intuition, and re-routing our path and our own map to bring forward our higher self and a higher standard in what we deserve in life.

What the F card? My intuition is very strong. My story is to show you that we all want to follow the yellow brick road and chase our own rainbow. Did you know that your life could change in a split second? This book comes from my intuition.

I was chubby growing up, and now I love health and fitness and most of all, food. You name a diet, I've tried it. Want a quick fix with a pill or a fad? No! You need to work hard, and the results will follow. What works for me is a 100% CARNIVORE diet.

So, what I've written above was meant to be a foreword but after I wrote it, I was told a foreword is written by someone who is close to you and had a part to play in helping. Ha-ha.

The best way to describe me is a little left of field and I won't follow rules. My book is about what's right for you! So, I decided to keep it.

> **I am the girl next door.**
> **I laugh at myself way more than I should.**
> **I am a dreamer.**
> **I love love.**
> **I believe in everyone and trust in everyone.**
> **I have the softest heart.**
> **I talk to the rich the same I would to the poor.**
> **I dress down more than I dress up.**
> **I help, not judge.**
> **I have respect and morals.**
> **I was a fat kid.**
> **I have a fat heart.**

At twenty-two years of age, I was stabbed with scissors by my first partner. On another night, he head butted me to the floor in a nightclub and then ran off. I believe he went into psychosis from being heavily addicted to marijuana, but I don't believe he was a narcissist.

However, move forward ten years and I was in a new relationship with a new man. I like to call this my learning experience (we've all had one). It's what we choose to do with the pain from learning experiences that matters. I was with a man who manipulated me, emotionally raped me, spat on me, and pissed on me like I was an object. My story 'THE GOLDEN MASK' is about my experience with a sexual narcissist.

I WALKED INTO MY SPIRITUAL AWAKENING. Now, I AM A STRONG MOTHERFUCKING EMPATH who sets boundaries like a boss thanks to these experiences that I went through in my younger years.

I now follow my intuition. I know intuition is an empath's biggest gift. My purpose is to help awaken you.

I want to help anyone who has been through abuse both physically and emotionally, to teach you how much strength and resilience we all have inside us.

I am here to teach you to believe in your dream no matter how big or small. You can reach the top and if I can change my road map, so can you.

I am here to help teach you how to remove any toxic people or energy from your life. I want to teach you how you can step forward with fitness, your mind, or a simple intention. How? With baby steps to bring forward your purpose with boundaries and meaning.

To all my sensitive empaths, from my heart to yours, YOU HOLD THE POWER. A soft heart is the new strong and sexy. FROM ROCK BOTTOM TO HEALING TO THE PINK ROCK! You are amazing. Follow your rainbow.

Chapter One

the dark night of the soul

The Path that Led Me to the Cover

It was black. I grabbed the doona from my face, uncovering my head, rolling over to check the time. It was 3am. I stared into the dark night in my small shoebox apartment, feeling the heaviness of the day creeping into my mind. I stared into the emptiness, thinking to myself, 'Not again.'

Sydney, Australia was entering its second lockdown in NSW. I lived in Bondi, and it was the hotspot at the time. Suddenly, all the past lockdown came crashing back into my mind, triggering the past trauma I'd experienced from the previous lockdown . The fear and loneliness it caused was too much for my heart, the feeling of anxiety being trapped inside my apartment.

'I CAN'T DO THIS AGAIN,' was the thought that took over my whole body.

Tears rolled down my cheeks. I wanted to see my family. I wanted to hug my niece and nephew, and I felt trapped. My family are in Nowra on the south coast, close to where I grew up in Bomaderry.

I broke down. I was done. I could also feel everyone else's energy. Everyone was sad and lost. Me, being an empath, collected all the pain. It felt like the energy of all the humans around me was being pulled from their hearts. I felt everyone's spirit drop a little lower to the ground with every step they took. I held their shoulders on my back and it was heavy.

It was my mum's birthday on the 24th of July, and I got up early as I always did. I am a member of the 4 am club. This day, I couldn't stop crying. The tears were rolling down my face from my cheeks to my mouth. I wiped them away with my sleeve as I took each step of my walk in the dark. I will still walk even if I'm sad, as it's all about setting up for the day. I was sad. I couldn't give my mum a cuddle on her birthday. I couldn't be with my family, and I felt sad with all the negative energy that was going on due to COVID and the lockdowns and what I could feel.

I walked the Bondi to Bronte walk, as I did every morning when I wasn't teaching group fitness. I headed up to the cemetery. As an empath, I have always felt a beautiful strong energy there. It's the emotion of connecting a conversation to the Universe that answers you back, a feeling of stillness, a feeling that opens my heart to be able to speak. It's the silence, the water, the open air, and the sunrise that greets me when I walk. I know some magical people have passed, yet their spirits are still living.

Let's not bring up the COVID-19 1.5-meter signs flashing in my eyes while I'm creating the emotional stage for you. Ha-ha. It was dark and I liked to keep it that way while I walked so I could enjoy the moon. I'm sure Bondi readers can relate. It's the most magical part of this walk that connects the walking path to the graveyard path. It's the ocean, the sunrise, the open views, and the overlook of the magical world we live in, and then boom, let's chuck a COVID-19 1.5 meters sign right in the middle. Let it flash like a Christmas tree in March.

As I got to the cemetery, there was this magical bench placed so that it provided a disconnect from people walking past. I sat looking out to this beautiful world, waiting for the sun to rise as tears fell from my eyes. I put my hand on my heart and I spoke from it. I spoke to the Heavenly Father, the Universe, 'I NEED HELP.' Everything is too much. I was so overwhelmed by too much traffic coming in, combined with the energy of the world enduring this lockdown. Anxiety was affecting me. 'Please guide me to my path,' I asked.

As the day went on, so did my tears. I couldn't even bring myself to call my own Mum on her birthday. I took myself to the Bondi hill to sit and take in the ocean, as my emotional fatigue was taking over my soul. I tried writing HAPPY BIRTHDAY, but I just broke down as I felt so drained, sad, and lost.

Finally, the flowers I sent her turned up at her door as she messaged me in her happy mummy's way, 'THANKS FOR THE FLOWERS KIMMY.' I felt relieved I could let this day pass. I always say to people who need to hear it, 'If you are having a hard day, this time shall pass.' I had to pull myself together to practice what I preach; I knew I would be okay. I was just having a moment.

That afternoon, my phone rang. It was my mum ringing me on her own birthday. She knows if I'm quiet something isn't right, and well Mum being mums, she was spot on. My mum and my family weren't in lockdown in Nowra at the time.

I broke down. 'I can't do this anymore. I'm sorry. I haven't wished you a happy birthday. I haven't been able to get words out,' I cried.

By the end of the conversation, we were laughing our arses off about a silly comment or smart-arse joke one of us had made. Then, we talked about her having a big night of nothing on her birthday wearing her dressing gown. I mean, who doesn't love a dressing gown? This was a normal conversation for us as a family. It is a funny one.

The next morning, I woke up early with extra fat puffy eyes from crying the day before and off I went for my walk. I needed to connect with the Universe to balance myself, get grounded, and set myself up for my day. I feel once I've done this, my soul is balanced, and my body and mind know and react in a positive way.

If you are an empath and have never walked up towards the cemetery on the Bondi to Bronte walk, put it on your bucket list and you will understand what

I mean. The feeling and connection are magical, and I'd love to know about the feelings you collect, so please let me know.

As I got myself back up to my front row seat for the sunrise at the same time, same place with no one around, I sat and spoke to the Heavenly Father. It was my country soul that wasn't okay. I felt trapped in the life I was living. I wished I had a van I could jump into and set my soul free. Sydney is fast, and my job and teaching group fitness was fast. I give out a great deal of energy when I teach, I give from my heart, my soul, and my body. Some days, I have nothing to give to me. Yes, I am blessed, and I love my job, but I needed to protect myself and my heart and put myself first. I am number one. Well, we tend to help others first. I felt that this was not serving me. During the lockdowns, my balancing act was slowly starting to tip and the only direction I was tipping was headfirst.

I was reminded of COVID-19 with every step I took. There were 1.5-meter signs, the bloody news reporters outside my front yard with a camera crew, and the COVID-19 drive through tent on my door blocking the beach front views. Lucky me! I mean, this is Bondi and I pay a lot of money for a shoe box property and a beach, not the COVID-19 drive through. Ha-ha.

I needed to be free so my prayers for help got a little louder. 'Guide me out of this feeling of being trapped. Guide me to a place that will settle me and take me away from this pain in my heart,' I asked.

The two-week lockdown got extended! This lockdown wasn't going anywhere fast. I was trapped. Things got too much for me with life. My work life as a nanny doubled, even though the gyms had closed. I wasn't teaching group fitness anymore, which was my fun. What you need to know about me is that I am an extroverted introvert. I am only 25% extroverted, and that's the person that my TikTok followers and group fitness classes see.

I love teaching body pump and RPM (cycle class) so much. It's my happy place. A place where I can unleash my creative energy with extra loud music, letting all my worries out and what us group fitness people do best, laugh while staying fit. It keeps me balanced when I'm not over doing it. Well, that was taken away from me thanks to the COVID-19 lockdowns.

All my energy went into my other job as a nanny, so my balancing act wasn't so balanced anymore. It was tipping over until I fell flat on my face. I was pushed over headfirst.

I was done with homeschooling, as it wasn't my thing. iPads aren't my thing either and that's what I was sitting with, watching children's emotions change while their heads were stuck in an iPad. Seeing them trying to learn was heartbreaking and they were not even concentrating, just sucking up dopamine, becoming addicted to the technology like zombies. This was happening to the kids, but I could also see it happening in the world around me and in myself. I felt my soul being sucked out by this iPad. It is a drug, it's ruining lives. These children do not understand why their emotions are swimming all around the place, and it's no one's fault. I could feel what was going on in this world and the energy shift from everyone was low. I found trying to pour from my extra big warm mug of Milo that wasn't full anymore was extremely difficult. 'WE CAN'T POUR FROM AN EMPTY CUP!'

The next day at my work as a nanny, my cup was empty. I felt like I had no heart, no soul, no warm milk, and no Milo left to give. I was back with the children I looked after who were my two little friends. I was trying to help them through this time where they needed me as much as I needed them. The little boy wasn't coping well, and his emotions were running wild. His soft heart couldn't explain the hurt of isolation and his dopamine was being sucked out of him from homeschooling. Previously, the home was a 'no technology space,' which I personally support. However, this meant that he wasn't familiar with using iPads and I saw a shift in his personality.

We were on a little food break in the kitchen, as I was trying to help him with some food after a frustrating event he had just had. He unleashed a punch straight to my nose. I froze. I couldn't move as streams of tears came flooding down my face. My hands covered my face as I closed off, and I fell to the floor. In my mind, I was taken back to a time when my head hit the dance floor as my first boyfriend head butted me in the nose and mouth, knocking my two front teeth. I opened my eyes to see him as he ran away from me, heading to the door of the night club. A few people came down to me to see if I was okay. I was shaking and crying. I brought myself back to the present as flashbacks started entering my mind.

Violence was too common in my past, and I had never revisited it or relieved it or ever wanted to. I'd blocked it all out. Obviously, people I'm close with know it's happened , but I've never flinched or thought of any emotion when I've spoken about it. It just flows out of my mouth like it's a normal event.

The flashes continued as I drove home. I'd be cooking dinner and over a period of three days, I was getting flashbacks in ways I couldn't explain. I'd never experienced the feelings of pain and floods of tears before. I'd never once thought of these moments of anger, hurt, and pain that were buried inside me and they hit me hard.

we can't pour from an empty cup

Chapter One: The Dark Night Of The Soul

I remember myself at twenty-two with my first boyfriend, when we came home from a night out and I could feel he was going to get angry. It was his cycle of abuse I was trapped in. I went to sleep in the lounge room, and he pulled me by my hair and dragged me across the kitchen floor, grabbing scissors on his way into the bedroom. There, he pushed me on the bed and attacked me twice. He got my hand as I went into fight mode. Then he went to punch my head with his hand, he missed, and his fist went straight through the wall. I got out from underneath him, and bolted outside in my g-string and his shirt, running to his best mate's house to get help.

I could feel us having the conversation of him telling me I was dumb and using condescending language while he spoke to me, believing I had no voice. His words made me believe this bullshit as I'd been spoken to like this a few times in my life. It was common and familiar.

I remember my mum yelling at her partner when I was a teenager. She had split from my real father when I was twelve. I recall yelling at them to shut up, but he didn't stop. This was an ongoing sound I heard, and it caused a great deal of pain in me that I was too young to understand. I remember I jumped up out of my bed, ran upstairs, and punched this man in the head. When I was fifteen, he kicked me up the arse, so I called the police. This experience was soon to become one of my triggers, as I'd lived with it nightly growing up - the yelling, violent abuse.

I was feeling sad, remembering the moment I realised I'd fallen in love with a sexual narcissist who used my heart and generous nature to be a sex slave and a worthless object. Then, after we broke up, I saw him driving past me in Bondi, laughing at me while I got on the bus. It was the smirk of a narcissist, and I thought to myself, 'Why so evil?'

The conditioning from my past made violent abusive relationships seem normal to me. Becoming involved with a narcissist seemed natural. I was chasing a love that felt familiar. I was mirroring my inner trauma and demons, and needed any love to feel wanted. I didn't know 'my worth'.

MOMENTS THAT TRIGGER US ARE WHERE WE NEED HEALING.

I was in THE DARK NIGHT OF THE SOUL as I sat on my own. I was broken. I started staring towards the ceiling and I couldn't move. The pain I was feeling just made me break and cry. The flashbacks I was experiencing caused me to ask myself some serious questions. Why did this all happen to me? What did I do wrong? Who did I hurt? I started telling myself 'A STORY.' It was the same story I told myself from when I was a young sixteen-year-old girl.

The Path that Led Me to the Cover

It was an ongoing battle I had from when I was a fat kid at school. I remember kids yelling 'Quick, here comes Kim. Run!' In primary school, boys called me 'fat' and walked past me saying, 'Hi Jenny Craig'. In high school, no boy ever noticed me as I was overweight. I was always reserved, and I put a wall up to protect myself and stop any kind of male attention coming in. Being overweight made me turn into a people pleaser, as that was the only way I knew how to be accepted. The feeling I became committed to was always making sure other people felt happy, so the attention wasn't on me. I wanted to be skinny, I wanted to feel pretty - not understanding at the time, I was more than just looks.

That dark of night pulled me back to painful places in my past, and I was forced to sit in the pain of what I had never healed. It was then I realised I had been treated like shit from every man I'd met, so I sat there crying. I told myself that same story. I didn't deserve love.

I dropped to my bed and prayed.

SING IT - *TITANIUM* - DAVID GUETTA / SIA

Chapter One: The Dark Night Of The Soul

notes

Chapter Two

spiritual awakening

The next morning, I went on my walk. The sun was showing its light, shining in my eyes as I listened to the songs I'd written in my book. You will see that I love music as I take you along my path. I started setting myself a daily intention on how I would get myself through each day. I set myself a few small boundaries of what I needed to do to protect my heart during this time.

As I got up towards the cemetery, I felt a soft push of someone saying, 'Why aren't you writing? You have never finished your story.' I froze. I started feeling my hairs stand up on my skin, my heart started feeling at ease, and my soul started feeling calm. I began getting signs. It was my intuition. All the questions I'd been asking the Heavenly Father were being answered. I felt my angels. I was being drawn to my path of writing and creativity. Knowing this would re-balance me, as I was not letting my creative side out when I taught. Being creative is something I love. Writing from my heart is my passion! I wanted to write my story and help others. It's something that I feel I was called to do. I walked back home past Woolworths in Bondi, and I grabbed a notebook and some extra bright pens.

This is how my story began.

You can use your pain, anger, loneliness, or even sometimes words as fuel to awaken a dragon that's inside you. Once you come back from rock bottom, you are unstoppable. You are the person no one will ever fuck with. I hope my story shows you how incredible you are, and how much strength and power we all have inside of us. I believe in you.

I finally realised the only person I was hurting was myself, so I grabbed all my anger, pain, and depression, held it in my hand and told it to fuck off. I had a moment with myself, and recognised that if I could hold so much anger inside of me over someone else's actions, imagine how much I could retrain my brain to have so much love and light for myself. So, I flipped it on its head.

My pen started hitting the paper, feeling the freedom of my emotions, thoughts, and creativity being released. It was magical. It was at this moment that all my prayers for help and guidance had been answered. My thoughts started filling the paper with this beautiful flow of freedom and connection to my purpose. An empath needs to hear my story, so they don't get trapped by the GOLDEN MASK and the emotional web and abuse the way I did. I hope I can teach my empaths a few of the most incredible, most powerful tools we own: our intuition, and the importance of setting boundaries.

It was the 8th of August 2021, and the spiritual world was overpowering my life and my TikTok news feed. I feel it was all sent to me as a blessing. The Universe was working overtime, as I felt the energy of people with heavy shoulders trying to adapt to this 'new normal.'

Not knowing if this was a good shift or bad shift, people were feeling the change, even if they couldn't explain what it was. As I was going through my awakening, I felt myself being pulled more towards connecting to my intuition. I was drawn to put pen to paper, not phone to phone as I needed to feel my writing and connection. The more I wrote, the more I felt the sun get a little brighter and my tears turned into smiles. I looked outside my window and said, 'Thank you, thank you for listening and guiding me!'

I downloaded TikTok during the first lockdown for some fun and laughs. I do love TikTok and yeah, I have a weird mind. Ha-ha. To my 17.6 k followers, you are welcome. Even though I loved it, TikTok was becoming too much for me while I was going through this huge change, so I deleted it for two weeks to reset my soul, ground myself, and let beautiful new energy in. This was when I started diving into the ocean daily. I never once thought to dive into the ocean on a winter's day (incredible). This cold therapy awakened my soul, helping it to be mint again and I was being pulled to do these new behaviours. The ocean called me.

It's very important to take time out and remove yourself from the phone world. We live in this beautiful place, and yet we don't take the time to capture it with our hearts. I watch people sitting taking photos of the sunrise while in the moment. Their moment disappears as they are too busy trying to edit and post it. That's a no from me. Ha-ha. Rant over.

I turned the TV OFF! It's full of bullshit that brainwashes us. I started seeing the media and COVID-19 vaccines becoming a little off-putting, thinking to myself something isn't sitting right with my gut and what's happening around the world. I will do my own research. There was way too much crap happening and I didn't want to be a part of it. The Universe was giving me all these answers. The media and the government narratives weren't supporting MY PURPOSE.

I feel asking yourself questions is the first thing someone does when they go through a spiritual awakening. Finding answers to questions like, why am I here? What is my life about? Am I living the best life for me? It feels like your spirit has lifted and you finally see all your inner beauty. It's about awakening the person inside that's been there all along, and it's about believing in yourself, your capabilities, and trusting your higher self.

Looking at my life like this, I realised that all I was doing was supporting others. Feeling the anxiety I get from this, Sydney life wasn't working for me.

Once you come back from rock bottom, you are unstoppable.

You are the person no one will ever fuck with.

I pulled all my past apart, examining the trauma, experiences, and behaviour patterns that got me to where I was at that point in my life. My dating experiences were coloured by the demons I was carrying inside.

Thank you for coming on my personal journey as I take you from my heartache, pain, and trauma to the beautiful place we call healing. We can change our map from a dark and treacherous tunnel as we follow it to the baby pink flower fields of beautiful magic.

As a super empath, I knew I was being pulled towards signs that I had the power all along, and this power was my INTUITION. As a super empath, we have superpowers, and we all need extra tools we can use. It's all about sitting with your thoughts and questions with stillness, which I will tap into a bit later.

How do you know if you've been through a spiritual awakening?

Lonerwolf describes it as first we walk through the shadows of death. We feel we are removed from this world. The soul is crying for freedom. We see lies and illusions of this world.

The part I find so interesting is that it happens to old souls or soft temperament empaths.

Your twin flame guides you when you ask for help.

Noise! I'd walk around and hear so much noise. Everyone appeared to be bickering with one another. They seemed too busy, bitchy, and edgy. That's what I mean. You can see people, and it's like you are watching a movie from another dimension. I see the fake laughs and emotions people show when most aren't really feeling that way.

I've always seen puzzles, patterns, and signs from the Universe but now it had become clearer. I saw my past and knew how I could fix my future.

I decided that I was number one from now on, and I would follow my intuition and let it take me to where I need to be. When you step into a spiritual awakening, you trust yourself more. I had a lot of hate and anger from the period that I refer to as being the dark of night. I now know we need to have just as much forgiveness within us to bring the magic towards us.

Why does someone experience the dark of the night? Past trauma was my trigger, then the icing on the cake (YUM) was lockdown. Some go through it after a car accident, or a major trauma they have experienced in their life. Sometimes, it can be the straw that breaks the camel's back. I genuinely believe spiritual awakenings

The Path that Led Me to the Cover

happen for people who are strong enough to look within themselves and heal to experience a new way of being. Looking back at my past and the events that led to the traumas I'd experienced, I realised that I'd never dealt with any of them, I'd just fluffed off and didn't heal or think I even needed to. To the people who know me, I appear very carefree and extra fluffy. Dealing with trauma and digging up the painful experiences that caused it is very confronting. I'd put a Band-Aid on it. Many people try and escape their trauma, and medicate their pain through addictions - whether that be drinking, smoking, drugs, gambling, sex, and even online shopping. All of these things can be from a trigger going into a trauma response. People don't realise that what we do and the unhealthy habits we form are a way of avoiding the pain from our past experiences and trauma.

In lockdown, the Universe said, 'Hey, you need to sit with your own thoughts and I'm going to make you feel very uncomfortable. I am going to pull all your past triggers, enabling you to do your shadow work and have some healing. Then, you can skip for the rest of your life.' I guess I am grateful for the lockdown in this sense.

I had held a lot of anger within me. This anger wasn't always towards other people; it was towards myself for letting people treat me this way. I have noticed the kinder I am on myself, the less stress I have and the better my days become.

I had to let it go, and forgive every person and situation that had caused me harm because forgiveness made me stronger. If we hold on to this pain and anger, the only person we are damaging is ourselves. These experiences in my life have led me to my purpose. I am finding the answers to questions like, What am I living my life for? What gives me joy and fulfillment?

The answer is helping to educate young girls who might be in a relationship with domestic violence and/or experiencing emotional abuse. I also want to help my empaths, and encourage them to use strong boundaries and their intuition. We all need to realise that WE HAVE SUPERPOWERS, which leads me to the big one:

How to spot a narcissist and how to not get involved with one!

This is my favourite part. It's all about 'healing'.

So, sit back and relax. Grab a tissue, a cup of tea, and maybe some boxing gloves. Ha-ha.

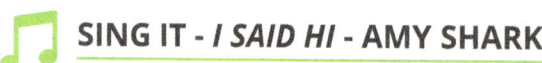

SING IT - *I SAID HI* - AMY SHARK

Chapter Two: Spiritual Awakening

notes

Chapter Three

the golden mask

The Path that Led Me to the Cover

'You are so beautiful, a breath of fresh air, not like other girls,' he said to me on our first date as we sat down to a nice dinner that he booked, as a gentleman does. It was the little things that night that made me intrigued. He was a gentleman who picked me up after work. We just spoke and talked about so many things.

There was something genuinely nice about the chemistry between us both, even though I wasn't one hundred percent attracted to him. I had it in my head to go after that different man that people always tell you to go after: 'the nice guy.'

He smiled and it melted my heart. 'I want to see you again,' he said, as we mirrored huge smiles. I smacked him on the arse and gave him a kiss on the cheek, and thanked him for dinner as we went our separate ways.

He messaged me the next day asking if I was free on Friday night, only a few nights after the first date. I thought why not? I'd had an amazing time. Our messages continued throughout the week. He would always wish me a good morning or good night. It was nice to have someone think of me. It made me become more relaxed as something so small and so simple made me feel safe.

We met up again. He picked me up from the city, and we went to a bar close by where we laughed and laughed until tears rolled down our cheeks. I did have a sneaky red wine and ended up back at his house.

We both loved music and we had the same taste in songs, yet one song jumped out at us as we sang it from the top of our lungs in our carefree attitude. 'This is our song,' he said to me as the night drifted away amazingly.

We had sex. He kissed and hugged me, and asked me if I was okay, then wished me sweet dreams and rubbed my back as I drifted off to sleep.

The next morning, we woke up and he was so respectful. Without trying to have sex with me again, he asked me if I'd like a coffee. I said, 'Yes please', and he made sure I was always comfortable, telling me to sit and relax while he made me my coffee.

'One coffee for Alexander, coming up,' he said. He handed me the coffee and kissed my forehead.

That day, I went to work, and I felt very happy. I was finally interacting with a gentleman who I thought had a heart. He messaged me every single day and told me I was the most beautiful girl in the world, and he would constantly remind me of the little things that made me feel like a lady.

Chapter Three: The Golden Mask

We would spend four days a week together feeling inseparable, enjoying beautiful dinners, having lots of fun dates, and constantly laughing. My favourite time was us playing the air guitar to our song. He was so much fun and young at heart, and loved AC/DC. I mean, who doesn't?

As we went to bed, he would rub my back and ask me if I was okay. It was this soft gesture that I loved.

The next morning, he made me a coffee, and asked me to sit down. 'One coffee for Alexander, coming up,' he said, handing me the coffee he made.

'I genuinely feel like the only girl in the world around you,' I said, and I told him how different he was and that I was enjoying my time with him.

It was the simplest of things I really took note of that made me start liking this man.

This was just as a beautiful loving relationship should be. We had a similar sense of humour and high energy level, which we both found very funny.

Four weeks had gone by when he told me he loved me, and he continued to make me feel special. I was hesitant to say I loved him, but I knew I had feelings for him. He wanted to spoil me in ways I'd never experienced. We went shopping the next day and he walked out of the shops with a beautiful bottle of perfume for me. It felt a little strange at times, as I wasn't used to someone making me feel so special.

We spoke and grew closer every day, and he learned so much about my past. He loved having very deep conversations with me, to the point where I felt so relaxed letting all my thoughts and emotions out, as if I was handing this man my life road map.

He would sit by my side or in front of me, leaning into towards me with both hands on my knees. Our connection felt close, soft, and genuine. He used to ask me questions staring into my eyes like he genuinely cared, inquiring about my past. I told him that I was extremely sensitive and that I take my time to warm up to someone, but that I felt I could relax around him. He told me he was sensitive also.

He started asking me sexual questions too, which was fine as we were learning about each other. His soft closeness was something different.

I wanted to have a bath one morning and he would run the bath for me saying, 'I'll leave you be and give you space while you bathe.' It was this I loved, as he knew I worked hard and needed some down time.

We just clicked on every level. As someone who is a little reserved with opening my heart, I felt I could just let myself speak on all levels of emotions or in any conversation. This man listened! He would kiss me even if he were just walking past.

One morning, I woke up earlier than him and wanted to sit up and have my coffee, so I let him sleep in. He got up and sat on the floor next to me, holding my belly while I drank my coffee. He just sat close, wanting to be with me. I felt so safe. Again, he asked if I was okay. He had the softest touch and his hands felt so caring.

The deeper the connection grew from our conversations, the better our nights became. These great conversations formed the foundation of our relationship's growth and time together. Our typical day was all about food, deep discussions, lots of laughter and then sex.

He was so caring and loving, protecting me and always making me feel extra safe by giving me cuddles and love. 'Sweet dreams,' we said, and then he rubbed my back as I fell asleep.

It was how I dreamed a relationship would be, as I'd never experienced anything so magical and perfect. My heart smiled. I messaged him when we were apart, telling him that I really liked him and that I thought he was an amazing man. 'I miss you and my morning coffee! One coffee for Alexander coming up,' I texted, then I laughed.

Over the weekends I spent with him, we would watch concerts that we enjoyed and loved to repeat. We even loved singing along to my favourite, the Chicks, or we would put some golden oldies on like Elton John. We would enjoy home cooked meals or prepare barbecues together.

Again, I had never felt this way before. It was the way I had always imagined real love would look like and feel like. We spoke about life, love, marriage, and kids. Even though he had a child from a previous relationship, he said he wanted to build a life with me. He wanted me and him to be together and for me to move in at the six-week mark, but it was all a little too fast paced for me. He always said, 'as long as we are moving forward.' He loved using this phrase, always being incredibly positive. I told him that we should wait until we get back after the ten-day cruise we had booked, about which I was so excited.

We spent every minute we could together. He said, 'I want us to be in a relationship. I want to spend every day with you. I love you.' He would always tell me that he loved me, even if I wasn't ready to say it back. At the time, I thought he was moving extremely fast and was a little pushy, though we kind of just clicked into place.

Chapter Three: The Golden Mask

As we sat down for a coffee one morning - he would still make my coffee, knowing it was my favourite part of the day - he started pacing back and forth. It was like he had a nervous energy consuming him. He said, 'I need to get us past the six-month mark,' like he was thinking of his past experiences. I thought, well yeah, that's the honeymoon period and he wanted the relationship to continue past that time. I didn't read too much into this as I loved the fact that a man wanted a life with me.

He was an older man, and this was something I'd never felt or experienced before. He made me feel safe and more secure every week, and what we had was becoming more like a happy fairy tale from a movie.

I took him home to the south coast (Nowra) to meet my family, for a karaoke night. I love karaoke! My dad shook his hand so proudly, and then the words flew out of this man's mouth: 'Craig, you have a very beautiful daughter. You should be proud.' It was a special moment for my dad and I as we are close, and I've only ever introduced him to one man before and he was my very first boyfriend.

On the way home the next morning, we stopped for a coffee. He asked for a cute photo so he could see me when I was away. We took a selfie at the local coffee shop in Berry before heading back to Sydney. As we got home, he said. 'I love you. Sleep well.'

He would always take cute pictures of the both of us when we were on dates, reassuring me that he was attracted to my heart and soul, and not for my body. To me, he had something so open and honest about him.

Around the two-month mark was when we were going on our cruise together. This was our first little getaway. The morning we left was so much fun. We got ready together at his place, as I'd spent a great deal of my time at his place and most of my clothes were there also.

Onto the ship we embarked. We were in a love bubble, and it felt like no one else was around. He would constantly tell me that I was the most beautiful girl in the world, always reminding me of that even if I was babbling about something silly that he didn't even care about. He just listened anyway, even if it was a story about how fast I go on my spin bike. Ha-ha.

As we settled onto the ship and had our walk around to get our bearings, our song came on. We were holding hands, and we stopped, looked at each other and said, 'It's our song from our second date!' It was such a beautiful moment, like a girly movie dream coming true. He looked at me in awe saying, 'It's meant to be.'

We didn't do too much on the cruise and if you've experienced one before, you'll know most people don't. Ha-ha. It was a lazy ship of dreams and food. My favourite part was that we trained every morning, ate, sun baked, and watched movies together. The movie Ferdinand the Bull was my favourite. We both relaxed around the pool, watching the big screen. He would always check in to see if I were okay.

It was nice to have simplicity. Most of the days we spent together were dreamlike, and full of fun as we laughed our way down the water slides like kids. Sex was on the rotation a lot too.

Even on the cruise, he would stop on his way past the fruit section and grab me a few pears to take back to the room, and I'd do the same for him. Well, it was pancakes for him. It was the simple things which made me feel special, and we thought of each other a lot.

By the end of the cruise, I had finally said 'I love you.' I felt as though I loved him more and more as the cruise sailed away. I said it to him as he was holding my hands, talking to me about our wedding and having a child. He knew I loved children and wanted a baby. I told him I was scared about giving birth. He said that he would create a very calm environment for me so I would feel safe. This was what I loved about him. He genuinely cared and always protected my soft heart.

I got my period on the cruise ship and had a sad day feeling down, drained, bloated. and generally yucky as women do at this time. He told me it was okay as he sat on top of me, holding my face as he gazed into my eyes. 'We don't have to have sex every day,' he said. He told me he would rather wait a few days until I was ready to have sex as he rubbed my belly. It felt like a spell.

'Yes, okay,' I said, as I wasn't really thinking of sex nor was I really in the mood for a deep conversation. I felt sad as he grabbed my face again, gazing into my eyes as he shook me softly.

'No. I don't think you understand,' he said. 'I will not use you for sex like other men.'

I recall thinking, why sex? Having sex with him was the last thing on my mind. I remember a feeling in my gut as I looked outside. I could not communicate back as something didn't feel right. His words didn't match his actions and the sex happened straight after this conversation.

While we were having sex, he started saying random things like 'Call me your Ferdinand' or 'Say I'm your little Ferdinand.' I never did refer to him as the character in the movie and I thought it was a very weird and a devaluating thing for him to ask me. It was strange behaviour. My intuition was speaking to me because my mouth couldn't communicate. I just looked at him, thinking how his vibe had just gone weird.

It became the Carnival sex cruise as we split the day around sex. He would always say 'This is what I do on holidays. I just love to hibernate and shut off the world,' as he pulled me into his spell and sexual mind.

As the cruise ship returned home, the love bubble slowly started distorting. I was confused. Why didn't he spontaneously grab me, hug me, or show love the way he did previously? When we woke up, he never made me a coffee, but would instead sit down with his head in his phone. Our lovemaking was passionate and happened daily to the point where it was all we did. It was at this time that I could feel him starting to pull away from me emotionally.

THAT IS THE POWER OF LOVE BOMBING

I HANDED HIM MY MAP!

I was confused but didn't want to give up on the relationship so soon. The cruise went for ten days and as soon as we disembarked from the ship, he said, 'I AM NEVER LEAVING MY SON AGAIN FOR TEN DAYS,' as he marched away from me. I thought this was odd, as he was only having him for a couple of nights a fortnight at the time. It was the first time I felt the energy of anger coming from him. I never thought I would feel that emotion coming from him after all that we had shared on the ship. He was treating me like it was my fault for dragging him away from his son.

That's when the Russian roulette had begun, and I was the dice he was rolling to work out what he could get away with next. During the third month from the start of our relationship, he took me to dinner, and it had been a while since we had been out after the cruise. I told him I was struggling with lack of the emotional side of the relationship, as I felt a little used sexually. Something wasn't sitting right in my gut.

The next day came, and along came the strong silent treatment from him, with basic short sharp messages. I obviously had thrown some negative words at him by saying I was upset and struggling. So, what better way for him to turn things nasty? Use SILENCE as a form of manipulation.

The following weekend was my birthday. He had planned an amazing weekend with my family and friends. He rang up a hotel that one of his mates owned to get a booking for my group and me. Everyone came up to Sydney from the south coast and as we got together, they asked where is ? (Let's give him a name. Ha-ha. We will call him little Ferdinand, just like he wanted me to call him.) My reply was FERD is not coming, but he picked me up once the party had finished.

That night, we had our first disagreement. It wasn't even that intense. However, he stormed off upstairs, flicking the light switches off and leaving me standing downstairs in the dark.

I thought if you have a birthday, and your partner pulls out of the plans and doesn't attend, you have a right to speak up.

The next day, he pushed me away and said he needed space, so I left and went home, giving him the space he said he needed. Even though it was my thirty-fourth birthday, he never once tried to make me feel special, apart from the contradiction that he wanted to play happy families. I didn't get a happy birthday out of his mouth, or even a card for that matter.

This is when the silent treatment started. I was feeling so confused as to how someone could be so in love one moment, then flick the switch and change personalities to one with a cold, cold heart?

After giving him space, I decided to message him, as things had just stopped with no closure. I genuinely missed him and missed his company. It was a mini break up. After two weeks, I invited him to come over for dinner and he did. He came to visit me for the first and only time, and we spoke as if things were normal and had a genuine conversation. He told me he loved me and didn't want to hurt me. I was so happy. It was the connection I remember we had, along with his beautiful gentlemanly nature.

His messages resumed with a 'Good morning beautiful.' He wanted to see me. The perfect, loving gentleman was back. This was the man I remembered. He invited me back for a nice dinner that week and it was a super fun night. It was like it used to be in the first few months of our relationship when we used to sing, chat, and laugh, and stay together for a few nights. We just stuck like glue. He said it was extremely hard to find what we had, and I agreed.

However, as the weeks went by, it started changing again, bit by bit. We had a strong sex life, as he was a very sexual man. While I loved this side of him, and enjoyed the sex, I also needed nurturing love like the love he first created. It was this type of love that pulled me in like we were a family.

It took me a while to develop a relationship and get close to his son. This man invited me into his child's life. I do have a reserved energy with new and deeper experiences, and I took my time to get to know him and the little boy took his time too. He wasn't sure if he could trust me and rightly so. Then once I bonded with this little boy, he started to bond back. I started getting a cute connection with his son, as he came and sat with me wanting to play more.

DISCARD

Once my connection was strong with his son, Ferds started pushing me away and not allowing me to sleep over when his little boy was staying. He used this little boy like a hook, and I felt more and more like a sex slave as this experience went on.

He would sleep upstairs with his son and put me in the spare room, and he would walk upstairs without even saying good night. It was like I wasn't even there.

I worked twenty minutes away from his house but lived fifty minutes away. At the time I wasn't in Bondi, but I took a job to be closer to him. I was ready to move, whether it was with him or to be closer to Bondi as that is where I was teaching group fitness. Then, one night I stayed back at work late, asking if I could stay with him. As the son was staying that night, his answer was a firm no, saying that I would wake up his son. My heart was sad. I thought, why would I wake up your son? This seemed strange, as he knew I was babysitting up the road and that I wasn't great with late nights. This man was STONE WALLING ME!

He only ever wanted me when we were in bed. The cute pictures and selfies he asked for had turned to more sexual requests, and the frequent messages changed to sexting. He always just needed a fuck, and he would message me if I were heading to work asking, 'Can you pop over for a fuck on the way?' I said 'No!' He was using me when the son wasn't around. The words and requests came out of his mouth so easily with no emotional connection, speaking to me as if I was just a slut.

We stopped hanging out together as he was stone walling me away. The last day we spent together was one I would rather forget. His son stayed the night before, so I went over when he had him for two more hours the next morning, before he handed him back to his mother. He put the child in his highchair and gave him an ice cream.

Then, he pulled me into the spare bedroom and made me suck his cock. He then grabbed my neck to pull me back up, then pushed me back on his cock. I was shocked. It was a five second quick fix of DEVALUATION, and no one got anywhere. He walked off saying 'I needed that.' Ferds had no self-respect for the child in the other room, and this did not sit well with me. His words 'he doesn't know' made me feel extremely uncomfortable.

This wasn't the first time he tried with the son around. He behaved like this child wasn't there. This boy was so sad. I could feel his energy and pain to the point he started walking away heading inside, as he knew it wasn't okay behaviour from his father. This boy was highly intelligent. I told Ferds that what he was doing was not okay, and I demanded that he stop and show some respect. He responded that he didn't feel right either, and yet again there was the disconnect between his actions and words as he kept trying to touch me. I crossed my legs to push him away and make him stop.

I wasn't myself in this relationship anymore and I started feeling exceptionally low and drained. I knew I'd fallen out of love. I was in a trauma bond. We had sex a few more times, as that's all this relationship had become, but he never once kissed me. I cooked him lunch the next day, but he never thanked me. I made him some overnight oats as he loved oats but as he ate them, he said, 'Awww. They just taste like oats.' Everything I did seemed pathetic in his eyes. Looking back, he used and said anything that would bring me down.

I tried to hug him, and that was the moment my intuition knew something was very off putting about this man. He took a step back to avoid the hug, and pushed me away as he was messaging someone else on his phone. His eyes were so engaged in the conversation on his phone, it was like I wasn't even there.

This made sense, as there was a weekend when he said his mates were at his house and that I couldn't come over. I knew very well he was lying.

At the sixth month mark, his behaviour was becoming increasingly challenging, and he was more demanding. He began to have this 'Dirty John' like vibe when he was around me. I went home and backed off a little, as I knew something wasn't right. I wanted to see if I was onto something, so I asked for a dinner date to test him a little and see if I'd worked his pattern out. I did this to see if the puzzle pieces would land in my lap as nothing about him or his behaviour was making sense. I needed answers. He agreed and somehow, I knew his response would be kind, but with no action or emotion. As predicted, dinner didn't happen.

He wouldn't return my affection, and any time I wanted emotional contact, his reaction was nice and polite, yet always very sly and nasty. There was always a contradiction between his words and actions. This was so unlike the first two months. I messaged him telling him I was struggling emotionally with him. I had given this man my soul and had no soul left. He had broken me. I genuinely felt like I had no life in me. I was hurting myself for someone who didn't know how to love. It was like he was getting off on upsetting me all the time and I felt that he had psychopathic tendencies.

At the end, I remember sitting on my lounge feeling lost, empty, and lonely. so I messaged him letting him know I was struggling with him.

His last reply via text was as follows. 'Yes, I agree we live too far away, work etc. We could be friends, but you have plenty. Hahaha', with an extra laugh at the end.

Our time had ended, and it was over.

BEHIND CLOSED DOORS

Passive aggressiveness was this man's king behaviour. He used it way too often to manipulate and bring my energy down.

In as little as three days, I had put the last few missing pieces of my puzzle together.

With me being inquisitive, I asked myself whether this man was a sex addict, a narcissist, or porn addict? Suddenly, the following words came up in my face. SEXUAL NARCISSISM: love bombing, devaluation, and discard!

I had fallen in love with a Sexual Narcissist. This man used **LOVE BOMBING** and **MANIPULATION** to get what he wanted from me sexually. Most of all, he used mirroring to manipulate me to fall in love with him like I had never fallen for anyone before. He was the real deal 'Dirty John', drawing me in bit by subtle bit. It didn't take long for the relationship to become purely about me fulfilling his needs. He cut the emotional side off as he slowly withdrew demonstrative touches and kindness; this is stone walling.

His game was very calculated and executed slowly and carefully. He withdrew any emotional connection step by step as if it was a game. I remember thinking his actions were as if he'd thrown a boomerang. He, the narcissist, gave out love, gifts, special dinners, and extra care, all laced with beautiful words. However, as the boomerang returned to him, he denied all of it. Ferds even went to the extent of gaslighting me, saying it was me who said all these things in the first place when I hadn't. He was good at gaslighting me.

In the beginning, he told me he loved me twice a day, then it became weekly, and then monthly. Finally, when I said, 'I love you,' he only replied with 'Aww!' Sometimes he would just pat my shoulder like I was a dog.

He continued to be kind, whilst any emotional connection was stretched thin between us. For example, his favourite 'play' was anything around sex or sexting.

He would usually ignore me, or he had this weird way of running off and saying 'bye.' Well, it was more like he was sprinting, as his psychopath mind was getting off with the adrenaline. This was him getting his source. His behaviour was so unlike the first two months when he would stick around and cuddle, hug me and hold my hand, watch a movie, or enjoy a meal. Towards the end, anytime I wanted to do something other than spend time in bed, he would agree to it, but he would never follow through and do anything. By then, everything was on his terms.

I am quite a simple and easy girl to be around. I only ever asked for one favour, and that was to be taken to the movies as I had two free tickets to use. He couldn't even do that. When I asked him why he didn't come to my birthday, a family gathering, he shrugged it off and said, 'I didn't want to.'

He had certainly put effort into starting a connection with my family. At the start of the relationship, he was so quick to come to the south coast and meet my family and my dad. He knew I was close with dad, and my dad did not deserve to be caught up in this sociopath's web, especially as he was undergoing cancer treatment at the time. What kind of sick human has the audacity to want to meet a girl's father with cancer to get sex?

Solving a Puzzle to One's Mind

So many confusing thoughts I had been experiencing became clear when I accompanied him to court to support him with a hearing he was involved in. The mother of his child, sixteen years younger than him, had taken out an A.V.O. (apprehended violence order) against him for domestic violence.

She said that he would say things very nicely but very nastily, and told the judge, 'He is not who you think he is.'

He looked at me and said, 'I took her on eight holidays. I paid for everything.' This was a form of control.

As I love psychology, I sat in the courtroom enjoying the experience. It was in that moment so many pieces fell into place. I had been reflecting on some recent incidents that just didn't feel right, but now the puzzle was starting to take shape and make more sense. I realised he was very passive aggressive.

He would mention his ex-partner to me in daily conversations, saying she was a narcissist, putting her down constantly. At the time, I believed him as I naively felt he was the victim.

Now it was clear. When he was talking about her and her issues, he was talking about himself! He often used to say that her game was taking 'small steps to be in control.' Now I see it so clearly, as this couldn't have been further from the truth. He was just describing HIS game the entire time. He lost control over her, and he didn't like it.

I found it so draining hearing him go on and on about this past relationship. I never understood why he spoke about it so much. Sometimes, it felt like I was only there to be an audience for him while he vented.

On first impressions, he was the kindest man and people around him were drawn to his energy. I was so disappointed with myself that I fell for this so-called family man. Yet looking back now, the warning signs were there all along.

He told me at the beginning that he was addicted to porn. I should have known this was a red flag.

I noticed an oil stain on his lounge where he would sit and masturbate. He said to me, 'This is what I do. I put earphones in when I watch porn so I can have more volume.' That mark on the lounge me feel dirty. He revealed this information to me in the devaluation phase.

He always said, 'I have to get us past the six-month stage.' It's interesting to note that a relationship with a sexual narcissist mostly lasts six months. If you are awake, YOU must break the cycle. They won't. The reason a relationship with a sexual narcissist lasts for this amount of time is because there are usually two months of love bombing, two months of devaluation, then the two months of discard. By referring to the six-month stage of the relationship like he did, he was projecting his insecurities. For him to say this was an indicator that he knew he would struggle to get past six months with me.

The things he did, I now see were to assert his dominance over me. He told me little lies, then would look at me strangely to see how I reacted. It was a look that felt evil. It's all in the eyes. The lies were never about anything big; they were so small that I started to believe him, and bizarrely he would start to believe them too.

Even on the cruise, I could see his game had started with him telling me to call him little Ferdinand. It made me feel uncomfortable and I never called him that name. I couldn't do it. It was **DEVALUATING**. This is what you call GROOMING. What a narcissist does is test you to see how easily they can bring you down, and how fast they can start to control you. The plan is to make you feel embarrassed and belittle you to see how far they can push. This step mostly happens in the love bombing phase to test if they can start to roll the dice. If I called him what he wanted, he knew he could own me, and his game could start.

Along with saying 'This is what I do on holidays.'

He was collecting pieces of me like a spider does, wrapping up and hoarding its food supply in silk, then placing it in its web and keeping it there for later. In this case, I was the spider's victim. This wasn't just on holidays; it was the six-month experience. They collect you! You become an object, along with the photos and videos.

One afternoon, I walked up stairs as he was laying on the bed looking at his phone. He looked at me as if he was asking 'Why are you even here?' As I walked to him, he said, 'Your attitude is disgusting. I wish I could tie you up for the day.' As someone who is soft and caring, it made me think, what did I do wrong?

One Saturday, around the five-month mark of the relationship, I went around to his place as we were meant to be heading out to his mate's birthday. As I got to his place, I found him sitting in a chair, appearing all down and depressed. He was in a diaspora deficiency. This happens when a narcissist loses control over their main supply. It's a feeling like a drug addict who can't have their hit. In this case it was his ex, and he couldn't stop talking about her. She was his main source that he'd lost all control over.

As we came home from the party and went to bed, he hugged me, and I felt strange because we hadn't hugged for a very long time. I said, 'You never hug me anymore.'

He replied, 'You don't communicate.' He used this as his tool against me because in the beginning, I told him I struggled with trust and communicating.

Later, he kept saying, 'Bitch, bitch, bitch.' As I dug deeper into this, it was because he was giving me emotion for the first time as a **reward** for the day we shared. However, the bitch word came in too quickly and took that reward away. This was **DEVALUATION** and he began to slowly stone wall me. As soon as the hug ended, he rolled over and demanded that I scratch his back. This was the **DEMAND** to bring back a small part of control he wanted.

I did nothing to provoke this response. I had spent the day doing everything to support him at a time where he needed me. It was a day we spent with his mates. It was a day I sat and listened to him when he was depressed, along with the time I'd spent sitting with him in court. The crazy thing with a narcissist is that they are very depressed people who always play the victim. They live in two separate worlds, and they can't maintain the outside energy when they are with you one on one, just as I can't maintain my twenty-five percent stage presence all day. It is exhausting. Remember, you will never please a narcissist.

Due to his carefully constructed narrative, he was never in the wrong, yet he still contradicted everything he said. Contradiction is the first thing you will notice if you want to know whether you are dating a narcissist. Keep a close eye out for this behaviour along with the feelings of shock and awe. He kept me so confused. I'd repeat something that he had said in the past, and he would gaslight me and say something that was so contradictory that I couldn't respond.

An example of this was when I was babysitting my niece and nephew on a weekend when he had his son. He had planned for the kids and I to stay at his place, or said he would book a room somewhere fun for us so all the kids could play together. That weekend came and his son didn't end up staying, so he threw it back on me telling me we couldn't stay. He asked me about the room I was going to book! Gaslighting me with a straight out lie to my face.

The cute photos and pictures he once asked me for turned into sexual videos and sexting. As time went on, his demands got more extreme. 'I put these in my private photos on my phone,' he said. 'No one knows I have this.' It's like they talk to you as if you are not a human. They have this guilt in them they need to share with you.

In the love bombing phase, Ferds would always lay next to me while we sun baked in the sun on his rooftop. He would always hold me or give me a simple soft touch. Once the discard phase began, he would sit on his seat with one leg crossed on his lap or with his phone towards me. His eyes would look at me like I was a piece of property, and his energy became dark.

One afternoon, we were in a very intense sexual moment as we were most days. Although he never got physically violent towards me, as he liked to think of himself as a 'good' man, he kept pushing me sexually little by little in small steps until I hit my breaking point. He told me to open my mouth while he hacked up a golly and spat in it my mouth, completely devaluing me with him saying, 'I thought you liked it.' He would always put everything back on me, so I rolled over this time and physically withdrew from him, making it clear I was not enjoying this game anymore. That was the moment he couldn't even hug me and ask me if I was okay, as he rolled over in a huff because he didn't get his way. I felt that I couldn't speak to him, as I knew it would have unleashed a torrent of nasty yet nice passive aggressive language from him. It was becoming obvious that something was very off about him.

Devaluation takes place in a moment of strong sexual connection and trust, like when you are at climax. A narcissist creates a high level of trust in the love bombing phase because they talk to you with so much love and understanding. You get pulled into a trauma bond because you trust them, and want the love and affection that they originally gave to you in the love bombing phase. All the beautiful soft touches reassure you and make you feel relaxed in the love bombing phase. When the devaluation phase kicks in, you won't be ready, and it will be a shock for you. He pissed on me once before in this same intense moment, and this is how they devalue you.

When we spoke the next day, I told him I was uncomfortable and upset. I remember telling him, 'Don't put me into your sick porno world without having a conversation with me about it first. Just "golling" in my mouth like I'm dirt was not acceptable.'

He didn't apologise and just shrugged it off to deflect any negativity towards him. His words were, 'You are so negative. It was just two people having sex.'

Ferd wore sunglasses most of the time so he couldn't make eye contact with me. His eyes couldn't lie, so he always covered them up. He wore them more after the love bombing phase. Narcissists tend to have this withdrawn look about them.

After he told me I was negative, he quickly took me back into the bedroom to get control back. With no emotion, he said, 'I need to finish what I started last night.' Here was the power and control returning as he pushed me onto the bed.

There were so many times that he tried to psychologically manipulate me. He liked to twist things around when I questioned him about things he had said. One instance that sticks out as an emotional rollercoaster ride was when I had left some critical things at his house (keys, phone charger, etc.). I tried to call him to arrange to collect them and he told me he couldn't talk, because his son was asleep. He couldn't walk away while his son was sleeping for two minutes. He then switched the conversation to blaming me for not telling him that I was going to lunch with my friend, and staying out a little longer than I thought. I apologised because I was so deeply wound up in his mind games that it felt like an apology was the correct thing to do. I can now look back at this incident and see how he was so clever at ignoring my needs, and twisting things to make sure I was the one that wound up apologising. He told me to go home, knowing I didn't have keys and not even asking if I got home safe. It was around this time I noticed the silent treatments were getting worse. He removed himself increasingly as the time went on.

One evening, I settled down to watch the football, thinking he would join me for some much-needed quality time. Who doesn't love a football final? He took this as an opportunity to take some time out, and left the room silently and ran upstairs. When I asked why he wasn't joining me, his response was odd: 'Aww, I'll watch football again when my son grows up', and off to bed he went, expecting me to follow. I stayed and watched the game, but as soon I got into bed to go to sleep, he grabbed me for sex. He would always tell me it was his JOB to get me off!

I couldn't even roll over to lay near him at night. I am not needy in that way, and I do love my space when I sleep but if I did, he would tell me to roll over or tell me he needed to touch me.

The following weekend, he was busy watching the grand finale with his "mates".

He used very small lies constantly, and this was a key part of his game. It was continual small lies and little moves until I finally realised, I wasn't fulfilling his needs anymore. Bit by bit, he disappeared emotionally. STONE WALLING. He stopped saying he loved me once we got off the cruise as a manipulation tactic, I suspect. He knew that by then I had already fallen in love with him, and he was getting the sex he needed when he wanted it. I did a few smaller 'tests' in the last month and his response was exactly what I expected: kindness but no emotion. This was his game – exceedingly kind, but incredibly nasty.

As he played the victim, it seemed like he was always crying out for help. I'm so thankful that I managed to extract myself out of the relationship as it was starting to have a very serious effect on my mental health. I had fallen into a deep form of depression from trying to please him and never measuring up. He would push me away and then pull me back in the shock and awe game, with him treating me like a sex object.

I felt so emotionally drained. I remember calling my mum in tears, not understanding why I was so upset. I would listen to music and feel so alone. This is why narcissism needs to be spoken about. It's like you are healing from drugs, and the damage they do to kind and beautiful souls is not okay.

The manipulation in the form of the constant silent treatments, constant mind games and treating me like dirt unless he wanted sex made me feel so lost, broken, and incredibly sad. As a narcissist, he was incredibly good at taking things away from me and letting me go like I was nothing but a piece of rubbish, leaving me feeling so alone.

Why is this so powerful? It is powerful because they have pulled you into a **trauma bond** from the **love bombing** they established in the first part of the relationship. Once they push you away, it's like you need a drug fix and you want to come back. This is not a healthy relationship. It's an addiction and becomes part of a cycle of abuse. The silent treatment makes you go crazy and makes you start thinking it's you. When they come back, you get your fix, and they start the cycle of abuse again, but you are on a high and feel like things are magical once more.

Whenever I tried to talk about my feelings or emotions within the relationship, he would brush it all aside. I remember after my birthday, asking him why he couldn't come. I stood up for myself and stated again about how I was struggling with the lack of emotional connection from him. He told me I was negative.

In the beginning, he was crazy about me and was fully committed to the relationship. He said he wanted me to move in with him in the first month of us dating! I said that we should wait until after the cruise. It was too soon for me, and I wanted to see how we went on the cruise together before taking such a big step. Interestingly, after the cruise, he mentioned he might get a housemate to move into the bedroom downstairs. I asked him what had happened to his plan about me moving in, and he told me I was skipping steps. He pushed it back on me. Then he said he thought I was moving to Bondi. This was another perfect example of **GASLIGHTING**.

When I would bring up the subject of us having children, he brushed that off as well, telling me to just be a step-mum to his son so I could keep my body.

His entire mood and attitude changed as soon as we got back from the cruise. I said, 'Our love bubble had popped.'

He responded with, 'Who popped it?' whilst checking his phone, devoid of any emotion or eye contact. The honeymoon period was officially over after the cruise, but sadly I was already under his spell.

He could manipulate a situation to make it out that it was me who wanted sex all the time.

Jeffrey Epstein like.

I never once saw love in his eyes.

I never once saw love in his spirit.

I never once saw love in his soul.

I never once saw love in his heart.

IT WAS A GOLDEN MASK.

 **SING IT -** *YOU SHOULD BE SAD* **- HALSEY**

Chapter Three: The Golden Mask

notes

I never once saw love in his eyes.

I never once saw love in his spirit.

I never once saw love in his soul.

I never once saw love in his heart.

Chapter Four

how to spot a narcissist

Through my experience with a sexual narcissist, I had to dig deep to discover the intuitive empath within enabling me to free myself from a false bond. Much of my growth and knowledge grew out of the pain I unknowingly allowed him to inflict on me.

I'd love to study criminology or physiology; however, I feel I don't need to anymore. Ha-ha. I'm stamped with the school of hard knocks. We need to remember that a narcissist is still human. They do not all have the same traits, or the same patterns of abuse or manipulation games. Not all narcissists play the victim. I can only go off my experience with one, however I can identify with the three-step switch which is **LOVE BOMBING, DEVALUATION, DISCARD.**

I'm going to try break it down as easily and as simply as possible.

LOVE BOMBING: People ask me, how do you know if its love bombing or love? What's the difference and where is the line? Here's the thing. **Love bombing** is a one-way street, and that traffic moves full speed ahead. It's the quick fix adrenaline rush a narcissist needs to get their supply. It's the over intense love; the saying 'I love you' so fast, with so much of it only coming from one party; the 'I want to be with you' twenty-four seven obsessive behaviours. It's the gifts, flowers, lots of dinner dates, the over cute messages about wanting to see you every day. This is as close as a narcissist gets to love and that's why it's so intense. These incredibly romantic gestures and the love they make you feel CREATE THE **TRAUMA BOND** WHEN THEY SHIFT INTO THE **DEVALUATION** PHASE.

Along with **love bombing**, there's **mirroring**. This is where they mirror your behaviour. They use your heart and soul to mirror you to get you to fall in love, so that you feel like you've met your soulmate. This is why they are so dangerous and powerful. They don't know how to love but they love to have control of you! A perfect example of him **mirroring** me and being a soft soul was when I'd look at something cute like a puppy or chubby baby, and with my hand on my heart and my head to the side would go, 'Aww!'

Well, you can guess what Mr Charming would do! The same but only until the **devaluation** stage.

Love is a two-way street. You both put the work in, and neither party needs to rush into the more intimate side of a relationship. Slow things down and take time to get to know each other before the stakes get too high. I remember telling him not to be so on top of me as it was a little too intense. That's when a narcissist will continue to **mirror** you, and then use it all against you once you are hooked. Those first two months were very intense, romantic, sexual, and fun with so much love involved. The intense moments and the feelings he created in the first two months became a drug, and guess what drugs do? They get you hooked! (Trauma Bond)

I'm not saying love at first sight isn't possible or you both can't fall fast, but for an empath it's important to take more time and listen to your intuition and heart and not just believe in words and fairy tales.

The **love bombing** intense talk is when they are collecting every detail about you as they want to know all your thoughts on every level, to the point where it becomes spell-like but in fact, it is creating the **trauma bond**.

They use your words against you. Mine was being sensitive and finding it hard to communicate. Even though I'd spoken to him very easily in the beginning, he then pushed it back on me, saying that I was very girly and my communication was terrible. He told me I was so up myself because he couldn't ask me questions. What he was referring to were the endless sexual questions.

Here's the thing: in the beginning, he told me I was the happiest person he's ever met. Then, they try to take all your limelight and pull you down, so you feel broken.

You think it's this amazing romantic love, however, they will use it all against you once the **devaluation** phase starts. So, the intense talks with the narcissist asking you emotional questions and questions about your past traumas are what gives them their playground, and they know what they are working with. This is how they know your weaknesses.

DEVALUATION PHASE STARTS

The main feeling I felt was the push and pull of the STONE WALLING. It's strange, because they use emotions and touches to slowly create a lot of trust. They give you their trust and you give all of yours. Then they remove one touch, one kiss, one hug slowly but surely. A few days later, you might get a kiss then it's spaced out for a week. Then slowly, there might be something else sacrificed like dinner dates. This is to keep you like a prisoner in their home. The spider holding his 'things.' You are his thing! They start removing emotion because if an empath has attached, the empath will come forward more to try to fix the issue while the narcissist keeps moving away. This starts the cycle of abuse.

What is a **trauma bond**? It's an emotional bond created with an individual during the **love bombing** phase. There is a recurring cycle of abuse prolonged by erratic reinforcement using rewards and punishments. So, despite what they do, you need them to give you that love bomb again because it feels good, and it becomes like a drug hit. The trauma bond is to keep you hooked and then you become addicted into their cycle of abuse. It's that moment when someone says that you need to leave, and you say, 'I CAN'T.' Being with a narcissist becomes an incredibly sad, lonely, draining, and empty existence because they take your soul, making more demands but using less love in the process.

There is proof that people who have been in relationships with narcissists have the same trauma and healing process in their brain as drug abusers do. So many people get post-traumatic stress disorder from being in a relationship with a narcissist, and it can take a long time to come back and recover from a trauma bond. I know, as I closed my emotions off for two years. However, we did go into lockdown and that affected me in my healing process too. Hey, Rome wasn't built in a day, but my great wall of China was! Ha-ha. My wall is definitely down now three years on.

The character traits of narcissism need more exposure and people, particularly young women, need to be aware of them. From a trauma bond, you see many victims go into a trauma response. Look at the Gabby Patio case. Here, sadly, is the perfect example of trauma response. She was sitting in the car going completely ballistic. The police had no idea she was in a trauma response. They spoke to her like she was the problem while Brian was standing there, calmly telling the police that she gets a little aggressive sometimes. The police were on his side, and they need greater education on this issue. How can police not understand the cycle of abuse? Two days later, she was dead!

That was a trauma response, and why did it happen? It is because the narcissist starts poking the BROWN BARE. They push and poke their victim, telling them that they are crazy. They push your triggers as they know your weaknesses, while using gaslighting and manipulation. The narcissist will use the victim's weak points until their victim explodes and yes, their victim does look crazy. I believe you could easily turn crazy if you are not strong enough or educated about this type of person.

THE VICTIM GAME: A narcissist appears to be a magical human being to the outside on first meeting them. The man I fell victim to had a lot of friends in high places and believe me, you would never put my story and him together. People genuinely trust the 'good' man.

Here it is. They live two lives, and they will never let the outside world see who they really are and what they do to you mentally, physically, or emotionally behind closed doors. Emotional abuse needs to be spoken about more. A narcissist will play the victim. My narcissist would put his ex down all the time. 'My crazy ex can't even shut a drawer properly. She slams it.' He must speak of her. I stood there wondering, why were we still talking about her?

Here he was playing the victim. 'She was young so I thought it must have just been her age, and me being a good man tried to save her.' He would say this on repeat to brainwash me. Obviously, in the beginning, you believe all his words as he's such a good man to the outside world. Why would he lie? Yet he was the one that manipulated a poor girl sixteen years younger than him for his dirty mind.

Not all narcissists play the victim, however little Ferdinand did all day every day. It got to the point where I felt like our six months was spent with me just listening to him putting his ex-partner down constantly. Be very aware of this when meeting someone. Putting past relationships and partners down is a massive red flag and it is time to say goodbye. It's a very covert narcissist trait. A covert narcissist is one of the hardest narcissists to spot as they don't play the 'look at me' card. They are calm and they play the passive aggressive victim game. I am only writing from my experience though, so I can't really attempt to describe a covert narcissist.

Passive aggressive behaviour was this mans 'king.' He admitted the way he wrote messages was FUCKED! He would often say to himself, 'Don't be a dickhead.' They dob themselves in.

He told me he would message his ex-partner saying, 'Our son is not a victim. Don't make out he's a victim.' He was still gaslighting her in emails, knowing very well that he was being very nasty towards this beautiful mum.

It can be so confusing and so upsetting if you are not aware of how a narcissist mind works. There's a disconnect of what a passive aggressive person says, and they do. It's like an emotional attack said so nicely, yet with a very nasty undercurrent. Many narcissists are great keyboard warriors. This is when you read messages like it's the truth and start to believe you are in the wrong. It's the twisting of the story that makes you think they are right, and you are crazy. Guess who says sorry? YOU! The narcissist gets away rubbing their hands together. Remember these people have been getting away with this since they were young, and they have spent their life lying. They are expert manipulators.

Along with the victim comes MY NUMBER ONE SIGN - **CONTRADICTION**. Why is it my number one warning? Because as an empath (not knowing I was), we pick up signs and patterns from people. Nothing ever measured up with him. The contradictions were constant, and the words and actions never made sense. I always said to my best friend, 'He contradicts himself.' I kept so quiet so often because I felt all the lies, and I genuinely couldn't speak. It was like my intuition and puzzle pieces were flying around in my mind and my eyes were staring at this man, questioning whether he was well or not.

For example, he always walked back and forth pacing, never facing me in a conversation, just talking aloud to himself as if I wasn't not there. He behaved this way often. It was as if he were nervous. His body language was telling me the lie and he knew he was guilty just thinking I'd believe his words. He said, 'I need to get a camera set up in my home as my crazy ex will think I'm raping my son.' So many things came to my head - like why on earth would she think this?

The real reason behind setting up the camera was so he could watch us having sex and keep footage of me. I never once saw it or saw him put the camera up, however he did say it didn't work anyway as he had tried it. So to this day, I still have no idea if he has more footage of me than what was on his phone. I remember he told me proudly, 'I have a private sex area. No one knows I'm like this,' as he slid one of the videos he'd filmed of me sucking his cock on his phone. When we split up, I asked him to delete them all. He agreed, yet I knew very well he was most clever at lying.

A sexual narcissist COLLECTS videos and photos to remember all their victims by. It's like they have won a trophy every time, like a serial killer who collects mementos from their crimes. They love to replay all the stories and scenes back in their heads, as they have invested a great deal in creating the crime. A lot of criminals plan as we do for a holiday. They dream about it for months and once the crime is committed, they keep photos as we do of our holidays to keep for our future reference. Well yeah, that's what a narcissist does with their victims too. He said to me one night, 'I've had sex with a lot of women' - again, like I'm not his partner, feeling proud of himself.

They are obsessed over control and power and think, 'Hey, I can look back at all the people I've collected whenever I want.' The cute photos turned into sexual videos, with him demanding that I send him a video of me climaxing. You do because you think it will make the relationship grow stronger and you love and trust this person. No, this is fine again in a loving trusting relationship, but when it becomes a pushy demanding sick game, it's not okay! They collect all these things for when you are **DISCARDED** by them.

CHARMING! This man was very charming, and the people who knew him would never believe a word they were reading, except for the fact he had a domestic violence charge against him from his ex-partner who I would stand side by side with and say she is an amazing mother who fell in the hands of pure evil.

A narcissist is not your soulmate.

A narcissist has spent their life lying, people watching, and wanting to be someone they are not, so they act and play the parts they like in people.

They use things they have learnt from their ex-partners to love bomb their new supply. These are the interactions with the ex that they can mirror and bring into a new relationship. A narcissist will use words and charm to get away with all these emotional games and yeah, they do get away with it. However, KARMA will come and bite their arse eventually, one would hope.

When it came to spitting and pissing on me, if this was a loving and respectful relationship, one would seek permission from the other partner and have an open conversation about it and what they would like to do. If the acts a partner wants to do are not spoken of and discussed, then it comes from a place of disrespect, filth, devaluation, and abuse as there was no consent.

When we went to dinner, I said I was struggling with him emotionally after the love bombing. He said 'I NEED MORE FROM YOU. YOU ONLY GET OUT WHAT YOU PUT IN.' Those were his words. You can never please a narcissist. They are so demanding, and they take and take and take until you break, and you have no soul left inside.

Then I laughed, because the only thing he knew how to put in was his cock, so I got out! Ha-ha. I'm funny.

DISCARD

The discard phase is when the narcissist knows you are onto them. They can't keep devaluing you because it must end sometime.

I noticed it more when the son spent nights at his house, and he used this time with his son as an excuse to put distance in between us. One afternoon, we were meant to be heading out, but he had his son. I wasn't at his place, so I messaged him asking him what the plans were for the night. His response was 'I just want my son to stay', then he told his friends that I just didn't want to go out and that I was like that. Well yeah, I am when you keep brushing me off. There is only so much a person can take.

The discard happens when the narcissist has a new supply - someone who is fulfilling their needs, when you aren't filling them anymore.

He came to me once and said this lady had been messaging him and that he had told her that he was already seeing someone. I know he was lying to my face, and he was cheating. A narcissist will twist every story. Ferds didn't care at all. He was onto a new rotation, and I was about to become his rotation (in his mind) so he discarded me to bring in someone else. Someone fresh who he can take supply from, as I wasn't satisfying his needs.

Hoovering: Hoovering is a tactic used to pull you back in or to keep you on the rotation. They have supply on rotation, and they will do all they can to keep the door open. Therefore, it's up to you to close the door and remember the **discard** is your closure. Why would they give you closure when they want to keep you hooked? The thing with hoovering is that many women get upset that the narcissist never hovers back. Well guess what? The silent treatment is a part of the hoover because it makes you run back to them. It's still manipulation. It's called GHOSTING, and this is what happened to me. I was the one who reached out, as there was no closure or reason for us to end things. After my birthday, the space between us became a breakup. It's a way the narcissist gets more supply and makes them feel they have more control and dominance over you. Here is the issue, once you are back in, the experience gets worse. Why is that? Because they now know they have more power and control over you.

Once we got back together, his words were, 'I knew you'd come running back. This isn't my first rodeo,' along with 'We will probably break up and get back together a lot.' He was DOBBING HIMSELF IN. That isn't how a healthy relationship works.

SILENT TREATMENT/ GHOSTING

Where do I begin? Any time we had a little issue, he turned it into massive issues with the old saying, 'I need space. I'll come back to you in a few days.' It was so confusing and frustrating. You can't have a normal conversation about your emotions because they don't care. They don't know how to love. They want you to obey them so anytime you speak up, it becomes a punishment.

An example I remember was when he suggested that when I was babysitting, I should stay at his place because it was closer to my work, and I wouldn't have to drive home late at night. Then when the time came, he rebuked with a firm no because his son was staying. It was always 'my son', like I wasn't in his family or his life, just in his bed when his bed was free.

THE NARCISSIST'S GUILTY DROPPINGS

What are DROPPINGS? It's a term I've made up. Ha-ha. The narcissist dobs themselves in. I always remember my intuition and how I just didn't understand what kind of weird man this guy was. They drop crumbs of narcissism all day every day. You just need to be smart enough to collect what they are dropping. IT'S

THEIR MAP! They need to tell people things the same way we all do. You know when you hold things in, but you want to share, and you always just burst it out - same thing!

Some of the examples he gave me were:

- 'My ex is a narcissist." 'She was young. She had issues.'
- 'It was just her age. That's why she was crazy.'
- 'I chucked the engagement ring at her.'
- 'I was standing here, and she said I hit her.' (The distance in his story was a room length away. He repeated this story to me continuously, and I could see him going into a rage if the relationship went on any longer!)
- 'No one knows I'm like this (sexually).'
- 'You are the most patient with me sexually.'
- 'I watch porn with earphones in so I can have it loud, and the neighbours don't hear.'
- 'I have a private sex part in my phone. No one knows I'm like this.' (THEY DOB THEMSELVES IN.)
- 'We are safe for S.T.Ds. I just got tested. Who knows who she was sleeping with?'
- 'It's my job to get you off. I read it in Men's Health.' (Not once did he read a magazine.)
- 'This is why I'm single. I'm too giving.' (Said as he was running up the stairs for sex. It was like I wasn't a human with a heartbeat, based on the way he just blurted words out to me.)

Let's look further into this statement. I'm standing there in a relationship with him, so why did he even say, 'This is why I'm single'? He genuinely believed he was God's gift and already had left the relationship in his mind, so he could love bomb a new or previous supply.

USING YOUR WEAKNESSES TO PULL YOU DOWN

When a narcissist asks you a lot of questions, they are collecting information about you! When you know within yourself an area you may struggle with, they will remember this and use it as a tool against you. In my case, it was me telling him I tended to be reserved when first dating someone and that I wasn't a good speller. (Ha-ha. I did have lots of editing help.) He then had what he knew he could bring me down with, and would say the following:

'You are terrible at communicating and messaging.'

'You never tell me where you are.'

'I don't know where you are staying.'

Apparently, a few of his clients did my RPM class and he told them to not tell me they knew him so they could keep an eye on me. So much control!

They use your weaknesses and where you feel vulnerable to make you feel less about yourself.

When I said I'm asleep at 7.p.m. and my phone is off, but that I'm up at 4.a.m. for work, the gaslighting and ghosting started.

Here are some other things he would say to me.

My favourite one liner was, 'YOU ARE SO UP YOURSELF.' He used to say this often, just to bring me down.

He would always say, 'I DESERVE YOU.' This phrase was coming from his sexual mind with his deep dark eye connection. He would say this sitting in his seat upstairs, often wearing his glasses, just gazing at me. I never saw love in his eyes. He wouldn't know what a spiritual connection was, and I don't think he will ever be genuinely happy.

My top tips when dealing with a narcissist
Never try to tell the new supply that the narcissist they are involved with is a narcissist. The narcissist has already told them that you are crazy, and if you say anything it will make you look crazy. The new supply will not believe you.

When being gaslighted or in a conversation with a narcissist, bring them back to THE PRESENT. They will change channels on you, blame 'the ex', or throw a curveball. Make sure you bring them back to 'We are talking about (the topic), not your ex.' STAY IN CONTROL!

A narcissist is not your soulmate.

My main tip is LEAVE. HA!

The sad truth with my story is that I feel sorry for Ferdinand because by writing this book, I've removed his Golden Mask for the world to see who he really is. I feel no hate towards this man anymore, although I did have for a year and a half after I left the relationship. I've learnt to accept it and forgive him and myself to move forward.

I won't be silenced on trying to help women or young girls understand these personalities a little more. If my story can stop one girl from wanting to kill herself and prevents a thousand girls from getting involved with a narcissist to start with, then I have achieved my goal.

FERDINAND THE BULL SAID TO ME ONCE, 'You are much wiser beyond your years. I need to be careful with what I say to you.'

'Yes, I am. You handed me your map the same way you stole mine. Thank you for making it so easy. I think you forgot I have a photographic memory.'

Letter to the mummy! I am sorry for what this man has put you through. You have done a wonderful job with this beautiful boy, and he is a very good kid. I believe every word you said in that courtroom, and am glad Ferds ending up getting what he got. It is his payback for him manipulating someone sixteen years younger than him when you were an innocent young lady. You were emotionally raped by a narcissist at an early age. Hence why my story means more to me, and I stand by your side.

Let's end this chapter on a funny note - I was at Woolworths in Bondi a year after we split, and guess who I saw? Ha-ha! FERDINAND buying flowers for his new supply - you know, the cheap $15 ones. Too funny. He saw me and I watched his energy go from a walk to a sprint of embarrassment!

 SING IT - *DADDY SAID SHOOT* - THE CHICKS

Chapter Four: How To Spot A Narcissist

notes

Chapter Five

the super empath

Over-Sensitive Humans

My story means so much to me, as the personality types that some people fall into were never spoken of or taught when I was growing up. I grew up with no understanding. My heart is soft, and I genuinely care about other people's feelings, emotions, and the energy of someone else. I can feel emotions as if they are my own. I also struggle knowing if I've upset someone.

This is how an empath feels. There is so much love and light in our hearts that we want to squish everyone, and give them all the love and healing we can. We want to sprinkle everyone with fairy dust. Then we forget we have our own needs, and we start to feel very drained as we have forgotten to set a boundary. Soon, we fall into a little hole because we haven't thought about what we need as a person. Sometimes a simple 'I'm so sorry I can't help' is the hardest thing for an over sensitive person to say.

I had no idea who I was, and it wasn't until after my experience with Little Ferdinand that all my intuition came flooding in, and my puzzle pieces started to come together. I remember just being frozen in motion when I was walking to work. I had a massive panic attack. I was shaking and crying. Not crying because I was in love and needing or wanting this man. I was crying because it was at that moment my intuition said, 'I WAS WITH A SEXUAL NARCISSIST!' My body was shaking, and I couldn't control it. I felt like I'd been raped for six months, and I basically was. I was so angry with myself for not being on the ball like I usually am with my gut and intuition.

Amazingly, in that moment two different human beings unravelled in a flash. I needed to understand who I was as a person. I've always known I felt differently compared to others, as I do feel people's pain and sadness. I'd collect this energy and take it home with me and wear it as my own. I get messages and signs coming in about someone as I walk past. I feel strong vibrations. I don't tell them as it's not my place and it doesn't happen all the time; otherwise, I'd do readings. I get signs from the Universe and pick up higher frequencies. On the other hand, I am quite gullible as I believe every word that's spoken and take words as gospel. I always tell the truth, so why wouldn't others?

I started doing a lot of shadow work to find more answers about myself. Answers to, 'Why is it that I need more time to heal and more time to recharge? Why do I love so deeply? Why does my heart hurt more than others?' and Why can people use me?'

Right in front of my eyes, I started making sense. I now see the world and feel the world differently. I am a super empath, an over sensitive person.

HOW DO YOU KNOW IF YOU'RE AN EMPATH?

Some of the signs are that you are easily overwhelmed, have a strong intuition, have a need for rest, have trouble fitting in easily, feel overloaded, are deeply caring, have a dislike of crowds, possess unique points of view, have boundary issues, and can be a little jumpy.

Now, we can be oversensitive and still not be an empath. You can be so over sensitive and feel people or be so upset over emotional acts, but an empath collects the energy. I can feel an energy from the Gold Coast to Nowra - that's around 14 hours apart. I know if someone in my family is sad, or I have a soul sister in Bondi who I'm so connected to, I can just feel her.

If you are an empath, this book is mostly for you to understand that there are some shit people in the world. WE CAN'T LOVE EVERYONE, and that's okay.

It makes so much sense now when someone asks me what it's like being an empath. I say it can be draining, as we take on everyone else's energy. This can happen anywhere from walking into a room or talking to an extrovert. Our battery can just die, and we need extra self-care and self-love to restore ourselves. We need to love ourselves like we love other people.

We can also spot a lie and see patterns in people. That is why I was so confused in my experience with a narcissist. I could see the lies and dangerous patterns in him. However, as an empath, I was such a believer that he was a good man. I couldn't speak sometimes, as my mind was working out his puzzle while my face was trying to concentrate on his words.

As empaths, we often stay silent because we hate conflict. So even if an empath can feel, see, and unravel the patterns or basically finish someone's sentences, we tend to just keep it to ourselves. WE JUST KNOW, and I guess this is why I am writing. It is so liberating, as I can express all my past and what I've held onto.

What is an empath? An empath is someone who feels vibrations. A person can be empathetic towards another if they are sad or hurt. Most good humans do have empathy; however, the empath tends to care more for other people and puts others' needs before their own. They act from the vibrations they feel off another person. We take it on our heart like it is our mission to help. It is a very beautiful thing; however, beautiful things can get taken advantage of and a narcissist can see an empath from a mile away.

Intuition is your biggest gift.

Boundaries are your personal protection.

Chapter Five: The Super Empath

We need to become more of a people pleaser, not an appeaser. There's a MASSIVE difference. A people pleaser is someone who wants to help others. An appeaser is a person who makes concessions to someone, such as an aggressor or critic, often at the sacrifice of principles held by the appeased. In other words, an appeaser will try hard to keep the peace at a cost to themselves, as they have a fear of getting hurt in some way. A lot of empaths tend to be appeasers.

WE ARE STOPPING THIS TODAY!

We will be KIND, NOT NICE.

WE CANNOT POUR FROM AN EMPTY CUP

My book is to help guide you through the baby steps to understand how we can protect ourselves as empaths. So, here are my 5 top tips.

1. **UNDERSTAND YOU:** if you are oversensitive, that's such a beautiful gift, but understand how you feel.So, if you're out one night and you are feeling overwhelmed and others aren't, that's okay.YOU need to have some space, and it is perfectly alright to go home.

2. **KNOW YOUR EMOTIONS:** Understand your emotional pattern and whether you are overdoing it. Do you tend to fall down after a few days? How many days do you feel good? How many days do you feel a little emotional? If there are a few days you feel you can't face the world, use those days alone to go for walks, swim, or if you have a family, try to get out and have a massage to clear space.

3. **BOUNDARIES:** Are you struggling setting them, and feeling overwhelmed or disappointed in yourself? Practice some boundary setting and you know what I'm talking about, because you can feel that little bit of frustration rise up when you haven't. Then, down we fall. Instead, set boundaries, and make time for you - and time for your soul to recharge. Breathe - 5, 4, 3, 2,1, re-start.

4. **GROUNDING:** Us empaths need grounding. It's so important, as if we aren't grounded, our hearts start to hurt, we fall, and we become off balance. I walk with my feet in the sand. My body is so

calm, it sets me up for my day. How else can you ground yourself? Some suggestions are removing your phone, going for a swim, doing yoga, being still, shutting your eyes, and sitting in the sun or in a forest to immerse yourself in nature.

I still, to this day, walk into a new room or a place feeling very reserved and calm. I read everything and everyone, and I can get so many signs that come in at once. If I'm not liking the energy, I just sit and be quiet, but if I feel a good energy, I can be myself.

The issue for a lot of empaths is that they manipulate themselves to take all the attention away from them, so they don't get hurt. They put up a wall to protect themselves like a shield and in a way, I guess my acting, teaching, and TikTok are my protection. I do this so I don't get too many people coming into my heart. But I'm also fine to talk about it, as I know how strong I am now.

My book is the first time I've allowed myself to be vulnerable in three years. This is the first time I've spoken out about my experience and my heart. The healing process, for me, is at the ending. Now, I feel stronger, open, and so confident in who I am. I know my worth and won't settle for anything less, and you know my favourite part? I've re-created my own map in the direction I want to go. Yes, I'm an empath, but now I'm an unstoppable one. I intend to block all negative roadblocks on my way, shining across the yellow brick road armed with bright pink slippers and a lollipop. Ha-ha. No, I didn't eat it!

If you set those BOUNDARIES, you will be a boss. The narcissist won't stand a chance when they are love bombing you.

Never underestimate the power of an empath: we have SUPERPOWERS.

5. **INTUITION:** Intuition is your biggest gift and BOUNDARIES are your personal protection. Think of someone you love. How would you protect them? Now, let's turn the protection back on you or your eight-year-old self. Make them proud and unhurt.

Think of a situation that makes you overwhelmed, like when there is too much traffic, a relationship is too much work, or when you have too many messages coming in.

Here it is. You have the power to stop this. Setting a firm boundary is in your hands.

A lot of empaths get overwhelmed from all the high energy or vibrations from other people. thinking I must do it all now for them.

Imagine and think of anxiety or being overwhelmed as a box you are holding, and there is all this collective energy coming into this box and you are the one holding it. Put it to the side as it can wait!

Remember, it's okay to not answer this phone call right now as you don't have the energy. Know you can come back to it. You have the power to give your energy when it suits you.

Set extra boundaries like a boss. This doesn't mean you're not being you or helping others. You need to understand we are people pleasers, not an appeaser, and there's a massive difference. DO NOT DO THINGS THAT DON'T MAKE YOU HAPPY, or that does not sit well with you.

I call it the hand arm method. When you are a giver, people will assume you will say yes and you'll keep saying yes, they start to take your whole arm while you're thinking, 'I only offered you my hand.' Don't fuck with this. Set your boundary. It's okay to say no. Like handing the chocolate mud cake out, but keep the Ferraro share! Ha-ha. This book has some of the best one liners I've ever read. Actually, it's the only book I have read.

We have such strong intuition, so we have an upper hand, but you need to tap into it and lean into where it's guiding you.

It was only when I went through my spiritual awakening that I finally had the courage to stand up for myself. I am strong. I am intuitive. I am honest. I am kind. I am caring, sweet, funny, very real, and very cool, but I am not perfect. I am still working hard on myself and my triggers, as well as my flaws. I can be a little bit silly too, but who wants to be the red rose? Not me. Ha-ha.

This is how I think now. I PUT ME FIRST. I will help all I can when it's okay for me to do it, but I will set boundaries like a boss. The more you set an intention for yourself, the easier it becomes to bring what you want into reality. Positive affirmations can be a wonderful help to get you thinking a better way about yourself, and to help bring about positive change.

As crazy as this might sound, I believe the Universe sent me a narcissist to learn to heal from my past, and help me to wake up to who I am. My biggest lesson I've been sent in my life was a man who stole my soul, so I had to rebuild myself with new strength and knowledge.

Empaths are beautiful people who are lovely, kind, and generous souls. Most of the time, they are too nice, so we need to remove a little nice and add a little spice. If you don't have strong boundaries and aren't clear about what you will and won't accept, people will chew you up and spit you out.

This is my affirmation for this week:

I am soft. I am strong. I'm going to put aside a day to ground myself. I won't answer phone calls or emails after 5pm. (This will give me extra time to balance myself, so I don't tip over the edge.)

I don't have depression. I'm just having a hard day as I took on too much yesterday, so I need to put my phone aside and spend my Saturday in the sun and ground myself.

 **SING IT - *WE ARE THE CHAMPIONS* - QUEEN**

Chapter Five: The Super Empath

notes

Chapter Six.

boundaries

What a new world of growth it is when you start to understand a boundary. How do we follow through with one?

If we look at boundaries, some may say what they are looking for in a potential partner: My boundaries or what I won't accept in a person is a big drinker or a smoker, or someone who cheats. Any of the above is a dead set deal breaker.' You could say the above are very simple ones, of which you absolutely will not tolerate when deciding on whether you will enter a relationship with someone.

Why I say this so strongly is because of my first relationship which started when I was eighteen. It lasted on and off for seven years. I didn't even have in mind any trait that I would not accept, let alone a deal breaker. My partner smoked pot and was addicted to it. Plus, he was a smoker and I hate smoking. That's a one hundred percent deal breaker for me now. Back then, I didn't even think about the consequences of what actions may come from someone who was addicted to such a drug at that time in my life, or the fact I gave all my love and energy to someone who wasn't even on my wavelength or vibration.

Why do we need boundaries?
We need to set boundaries to protect ourselves. They set us up for success, no matter what area of life we set them in.

What is a boundary? It's something we need to look at within ourselves to hold us accountable for our own actions. They help protect us when we get ourselves in situations, and create a foundation for us to be ready to come forward in our truth so we can be our complete self.

As an empath, we find it harder to set firm boundaries, as we like to put everyone else before us. We can be way too fluffy, so we just go along with the ride and agree to a situation so we don't create any conflict, whilst at the same time dismissing our own needs. This is why setting and keeping boundaries is super important!

A perfect example of me respecting my boundaries would be so simple now. When dating little 'Ferds', he would bring up his ex-partner way too often. My response now would be, 'Hey, thanks for dinner, however I see you are still going through some things with your ex or you still aren't over her, so I'd like to leave it at that. I hope things work out. All the best. Bye.' Looking back on what I've learnt through experience, him constantly putting his ex-partner down was a massive red flag.

And why does this sound so basic? I realised that I don't need to fix a man and his issues. If a person was healed, they would come to a date with an open heart and a desire to move forwards, not backwards, because they would have already worked on their problems. An empath and a narcissist would not become an item if a simple boundary had been set up by the empath.

A boundary doesn't always have to be towards a person; it can be personal. If you want to get better at 'something' in life, you need to set a boundary. Like maybe your friends want to go and get drunk on a Saturday night, yet you want to do really well in a marathon, so you set a boundary and say, 'No! I can't come out as I'm really focusing on this marathon for me!' A real friend will respect you.

A boundary I set for myself is putting my phone on flight mode at 6pm to 7am This allows me time and space to decompress from the day, and not get hooked into wasting my precious time on social media. Then setting myself up each morning. By doing this, I am respecting myself and my needs. I am putting my time first. I get up at 4am every morning, and I think this is where my success comes from. I don't go out drinking and partying. I focus on what's ahead for the next day, which in turn helps me move forward attaining goals and the life I want.

When you first start to set boundaries, it can be hard to get your head around. Just think baby steps. Small, simple boundaries make the big ones easier to set up. Start writing down weekly boundaries and intentions if it will help you. Write five small ones each week and stick to them. This will be a massive achievement, and remember practice makes perfect. Make sure you search within yourself, your life, and the area you need to put a boundary in place. Maybe you could ask loved ones who you trust for some ideas of where they see you are lacking boundaries. You can start by setting some goals for yourself. Intentions or affirmations can be along the same line.

A perfect example of a weekly boundary or intention for me would be to complete only 1 TikTok a day and film for 30 minutes maximum. That takes care of my creative side, and then my phone doesn't need to be in my hand all day. This is important to me, as I get headaches and bad anxiety from my phone. I'd rather spend my spare time outside in the sun or at the beach.

Before my spiritual awakening, I found myself walking away from conversations or situations feeling frustrated, sad, angry, or just exhausted, and now I can see the reasons why. It's because these conversations had no meaning, and became negative draining talks of 'he said, she said' or 'they are unwell' or 'they are sick'. I found my voice rising, becoming involved in the circles and repeating the language. I now put my phone to the side if it's a notification I see, and I simply won't participate in the discussion if it's not sitting right with my heart or I'm not in the right headspace to have this conversation at this present time. It's a boundary I set for myself, so I don't get wound up. We have a choice to say, 'This conversation isn't sitting right with me' or 'We don't need to dive into it right at this moment.' Boundary Queen!

When I set my intentions, I can remind myself every day and that will set myself up perfectly to achieve more in my life of what I want. I have set so many boundaries with writing this book, and all I have manifested is the finished product. I have not let negative or annoying energy in by simply not playing the game with a male, if I can feel it's a massive waste of time.

Write affirmations or your goal, and display it in a place where you will see it. Then, write some boundaries you need to set to get to the end. For example, I will eat clean and not eat ice cream, so I can be fitter and healthier while I focus on my marathon.

I also set a solid weekly intention. When this book was in its final stage, I started feeling too much anxiety. I then would start babbling on with extra nonsense that you would read and think, this chick is so cool and weird at once. Ha-ha.

Before I sorted myself out, I used to think 'I need to do x, y, and z, and I want it all at once.' That's when we can get so overwhelmed, so I stepped back and said, 'Right, set a weekly intention in point form.' My thinking became clearer, and I wasn't flapping around like a galah anymore. My weekly intention was simple: I want my book edited by me this week so I can get it proofread. Once I set the extra boundaries, guess what happened? My editing got done.

Boundaries can be on any level. It really depends on the area of your life you are needing them in. Work, relationships, dating, friends, or even family are just some examples where you may need to set some boundaries.

Let's use dating for an example. A simple boundary could be, 'I will not sleep with this man/female on the first date' or 'I won't go to a man's/female's house on the first date.'

What does this bring? Potential for a better relationship with more spark and curiosity. Also, you want to know that this person is on the same page as you and that can take time.

We need to stop handing ourselves out like flyers. Ha-ha. That's a good one, but it's true. Remember, you are the pure diamond, not the box it comes in. Oh, stop it! Another good liner. Ha-ha!

Looking back, one mistake I made was telling Ferd about my dad's cancer battles and my sister's experience in gaol due to being addicted to ice. Now, they are both four years free and clean and I am so proud of them both. Me being an open book, I told Ferd all about their journeys. This put all my trauma on the table, giving him my emotional map to play with. It wasn't to play the sob card. That was just me and my mouth. If you know me, you'll know I have no filter and I'm fluffy. Ha-ha. A narcissist would be rubbing his hands together thinking, 'Perfect. You will be easy to manipulate as you have trauma, and you are at a low point in your life.' They are very nasty people.

Be yourself and be true to yourself. People seem so fast to put on a front of how they think other people want to see them. Be yourself and just relax into it. There is only one you. Celebrate your uniqueness by being strong in who you are. You are valuable. This belief in yourself will help attract a partner who is more a reflection of you.

Match someone's energy a little, but don't walk into each date thinking 'He's the one. I'm getting married.' On each date, us girls can carry on like he is the one, and think this is going to end with a happy ending like it does in fairy tales. Take time to get to know that person and don't rush the physical part of the bond either.

Relationships

It is important to come forward with your truth. You can still be a boss and stay in your feminine energy, but if something doesn't sit right, say so. In other words, if intuition is pulling you from your core to speak up, speak up for yourself. You have nothing to lose. I never once said no to sex with Ferdinand, not once. This is why my soul was so destroyed; he was just take, take, take, because I didn't understand a simple boundary, speak my truth, or understand my worth.

I had not set one boundary about what was acceptable behaviour from a man. I didn't even know what a boundary was until the discard phase. That's when I said, 'Fuck you! I am stronger than you will ever know,' and I began to find my feet. For example, in the love bombing phase, the relationship was loving, respectful, and romantic, and making love flowed naturally. Towards the end of the devaluation phase and into the discard phase, all the softness had disappeared. He basically clicked his fingers, had sex and said Good night.' HE STONE-WALLED ME.

I finally set boundaries after I noticed this situation got worse. He ran up the stairs as he always did, and I sat on my own to watch television. I set up a boundary thinking, 'I'm not your sex slave.' It was weird behaviour from him and if I had of kept following him upstairs for sex, that would be me not setting any boundary for my self-worth! Instead, I stayed downstairs and kept watching television, as I wanted quality non-physical time with him. As soon as I went to bed, he grabbed me.

I thought I was worth a little more and I would not bow down. I now will never let a man fuck with my heart again, especially when it is as pure and magic as mine. I will always know my worth from now on.

If an empath has too much traffic of peoples' energy coming in and they begin to feel overwhelmed, they need to use an energy block. An energy block is a strategy that you can use to detach yourself from the present moment, giving you time to breathe and to gather your thoughts. If you are stuck in a conversation where there are too many people or the situation is uncomfortable, you can say 'I need five minutes to regroup' or you can easily say 'I need a few days to process this. I will get back to you' It is okay to put yourself first and set that boundary.

Remember if you've set small boundaries, the big ones should be easier to talk about. It will feel easier with practice.

I've noticed my energy block is that I always sing, even at work. I can be annoying, and I don't care. I never realised it was my heart protecting my own energy. Singing helps keep my vibration up, and pushes away any negative vibes coming my way. Apparently, humming does the same thing if you don't like singing but I say SING IT extra loud. Ha-ha. I think my old work mates and classes miss my voice.

Music is my calm, my release, and how I let go of stress when the world is too much. That's why I love my job. RPM is my happy place, as it helps me let go of the world or any collective energy that's bringing me down. I remember walking into class crying and not wanting to be around anyone, and yet as soon as that music hit my soul, my face lit up and the class was on. I let everything go!

RPM is the only place I can shut up and yell all at once. I suggest singing in the shower or the car, or put some old school love songs on if you need too. Do whatever you need to do to shift the negative energy.

I listened to Amy Shark while I wrote this. She is the only person who brings me soft energy so I can put pen to paper, and it's a magical feeling.

Also, start journaling to see how far you've come. Taking baby steps is my thing and lots of baby steps create massive achievements. Writing down something you are thankful for each day is a wonderful practice. Write it down while you sing. Ha-ha. You hold your own energy and remember: don't feel you have to give it all to anyone or any situation.

Let's use your phone as the perfect example of setting a boundary - in this case a personal one. I put my phone on flight mode at 7pm. Then in the morning, I won't take it on my walk because it's all about filling up my cup before work so I can be present for my job, life, or even a relationship. This boundary seems so small, yet it's something that makes my day amazing. The same thing goes if you are on a date or with a friend. Let's not be on our phones all the time. Learn to be present and value the time you are with that person. Learn to listen and understand each other.

I will not be with someone who is on their phone all the time. That's my boundary. I am not coming from a place of jealousy or not trusting; there's just more to life than what's on our phones, and I want to spend time with people who have the same values. That is a simple boundary.

People are so quick to judge me being on TikTok all day, but I couldn't think of anything worse than spending all my time on my phone. I set solid boundaries with it, unless it's one I've been paid for and then it becomes a job. I have done a sneaky advert for Donut King In donut PJs, an advert for a TAFE with Gordon Tallis, an activewear promotion for Runfastergear, and obviously a TikTok for a free Oodie.

So, start setting little personal boundaries that are for you. You are number one. When an empath starts setting more boundaries, we start walking around with a little extra swagger. It feels as if we've turned gangster like, because we have this tough gift in us that only empaths can understand. A lot of people do feel like this daily, so for an empath, it's feels pretty fucking tough and solid, because now you have more confidence in yourself. It gives you more control over yourself and life. You become clearer in what you will and won't accept, and I am proud of you for stepping up because it's hard work to do!

How different will your week ahead look, as you start putting yourself first and putting boundaries up to protect yourself and your time?

Also, look within yourself to work out what's going on in your life and in which area you need to set more boundaries. Write them down, and each week check your intentions. Be accountable with yourself. Did you achieve what you wanted to? My weekly intention and boundary this week is to say, 'Fuck off' if I feel the need. Ha-ha.

We used to think the power was outside of us when it's been inside of us all along. Caitlin, my soul sister, I am proud of you.

 SING IT - *YOU'RE THE VOICE* - JOHN FARNHAM

We used to think the power was outside of us when it's been inside of us all along.

Caitlin, my soul sister, I am proud of you.

Chapter Six: Boundaries

notes

Chapter Seven

the super empath and the narcissist

Think of a spider that has spent the night creating a beautiful, incredible web. Imagine the design, the shapes, the patterns, where it is placed, and how big and safe it looks. It is amazing. Then, along comes a beautiful butterfly, the softest butterfly of them all. The butterfly is so curious about this incredible safe looking web that she decides she wants to fly there for a few days. Later, she learns she's being wrapped in a cocoon of spider silk as the spider sucks all the blood and beauty from her body and her soul. This gentle butterfly can't escape. The spider then drifts off collecting more and more butterflies, and places them in the web for when it needs its next feed.

Sadly, if the butterfly isn't smart enough to know it's a spider web, it is doomed! I had zero boundaries, and had no idea that a spider or this type of 'web' existed. I love, I trust, and I see the good in everyone. I believed every lie that came out of that man's mouth. That's the power of love bombing and manipulation from narcissist.

The empath will feel sorry for the narcissist when the narcissist is playing the victim.

The love bombing and the mirroring from the narcissist is what the empath will fall in love with. Remember the narcissist is mirroring you!! You are magical. You hold the golden mask. Once the love bombing phase is over, the empath is hooked, stuck, and trapped in an evil tangled spider web.

This is what the narcissist plan was from the first hello. An empath is just a supply of whatever a narcissist needs for power and control. The game of Russian roulette has begun for the narcissist. They now hold all the power, and can remove their golden mask and move into the devaluation phase.

Why is this so dangerous? It is because the narcissist has created a safe, loving, and caring space for the empath, and what is it an empath loves? Trust - the biggest player in the start of the relationship. An empath loves feeling safe in a relationship, just like anyone else.

The empath is hooked, thinking they have found their soulmate. All the extra love and care, combined with the extra 'little things' like a coffee every morning for two months, really helped me become deeply attached to him. It can be the simple gestures that an empath will appreciate, and the empath knows that they will always do their best to repay the favours.

The Devaluation

I will always remember his eyes, as they are the window to the soul. He couldn't have a normal conversation with me without wearing his glasses. The crazy thing about a narcissist is they are very insecure. I always found it weird that he couldn't look me in the eyes when I was trying to talk to him about my emotions or feelings.

When it was him controlling and gaslighting me, he would kind of EYE GAZE OFF between two completely different worlds and personalities. I take this as the narcissist gaze of lies and manipulation. To the empath, the gaze contributed to why I was so confused. I couldn't say anything back in those moments, because I could see the patterns and the lies, and nothing added up. This happened a lot. An empath will see the patterns and lies in conversations; however, because WE HATE CONFLICT, we tend to not speak up for ourselves. I ended up taking notes for my book as a form of speaking up for myself. Ha-ha-ha. Oh! That is funny SHIT!

Once the empath starts to notice the switch - and I mean switching from holding hands, I love you, and I miss you to not even noticing you walk through the door - this is when the narcissist will come back and use a little love bomb. It's that shock and awe, the push and pull feeling that keeps the empath confused. It's like a game the empath is involved in. The empath will hold onto that connection; however, the feeling of connection becomes an addiction. This is called the 'trauma bond.'

Signs of Trauma Bond

A trauma bond is an emotional attachment that develops out of a repeated cycle of abuse, devaluation, and positive reinforcement. The trauma of abuse may create powerful feelings you struggle to make sense of, especially when abuse alternates with kindness and love. (This definition was taken from www.healthline.com)

You feel addicted. You are hooked and you stay because they fulfill your needs. You brush off their bad behaviour because you are addicted to the love bombing.

The sex will increase. That's all I felt we did - SEX! It wasn't always so intense to start with. I didn't enjoy it, as I wasn't in love and didn't feel connected to start with. Then, once I felt love and connection, it got better. However, it became too obsessive, to the point where we didn't share time together as a couple outside the bedroom. Why does this happen? Because an empath doesn't know how to use the word NO!!! I'm all for sex daily, if it's a loving relationship coming from both parties.

We need to focus on the importance of the word no. It's a NO, BECAUSE THIS DOESN'T SIT RIGHT WITH MY HEART OR MY FEELINGS.

It is caused by the root issue growing up. We want to please everyone to push away our emotions. To suppress our emotions, we tend to stay mute to save face. NO! Speak your truth.

By the third or fourth month, the narcissist becomes bored, and is already love bombing a new supply. Think back to the butterflies that are stuck in the web, but haven't been sucked dry yet. These are the women that he has on tap. They also have their fantasy supply, which is the main woman that they have the most control and power over. Many unsuspecting women cannot understand why a narcissist hasn't hoovered them back. It's because the narcissist has a higher supply of a person that they know they have more control over and can manipulate easily.

KNOW YOUR SELF WORTH: 'WE ARE NOT THE LOWEST DANGLING FRUIT ON A TREE. DON'T BE A DANGLER.' Empaths, please step forward into your future and slam the door shut on a narcissist. (Pink Rock)

The Discard

Generally, a narcissist has an exit plan from the get-go. The reason being, 'everyone leaves them', so they must spread the word that the empath or their ex-partner is crazy. Remember, narcissists are very insecure and depressed people who appear very clever to the outside world.

I remember when we went to dinner after the cruise, I told him I was struggling with him emotionally, and his answer was 'I need more from you!' That was a typical narcissist response. Driving home, he told me that I was just planning my exit out of this relationship. At that time, there was no exit plan in my head and leaving wasn't on my mind. I was just having a conversation about my feelings and my emotions. As we drove home, he ended up telling me his exit plan, like it was on the tip of his tongue and he was ready to leave me.

How characteristically narcissist! This is why an empath gets so confused. You literally can't have a normal conversation about your feelings. This man would then say my communication was terrible and push me away. What he forgot was that all the conversations that he started were based solely about sex, and anything I tried to talk about was irrelevant to him.

When it comes to sex with the narcissist and an empath, the narcissist has created a dopamine addiction with the love bombing. Again, the empath will be in a trauma bond with the narcissist, as they use mirroring of touch and emotions. This is when they make the most eye contact, as they stare into the empath's soul telling them little lies. An example of this was when Ferds continually told me he was oversensitive. This is him mirroring back to me what he knew I was. The empath is hooked again.

The narcissist gets his supply, and the empath gets their needs and wants for intimacy met.

This is when the sexual part becomes tricky. The narcissist has worked hard on creating the romantic love and trust in the relationship that the empath has now learnt trust and opened their heart to. Little does the empath know that there is a storm coming.

It's now time for the narcissist to devalue the empath, and the empath isn't prepared for the switch. In my case, it went from 'I'll never use you sexually' to intimately telling me to open my mouth as he spat the golly in. I was in total shock and disgust, and flew into absolute distress.

Once an empath breaks away from a narcissist, there is a lot of healing involved for the empath. An empath will generally not be interested in one-night stands, or probably not a new relationship for that matter; however, the narcissist is already in a new one. It's important to be kind to yourself and be kind to your soul and heart. Take extra time to understand that it was not your fault that you loved and trusted so much. Remember that you may not be able to get over the damage done by a narcissist easily, and it may be a good idea to get help with your healing. We are good people. It's understanding the fact that people can be shit.

Try to clear your mind, and nurture yourself with baths, candles, and soft music to rebuild your beautiful soul to the strongest it will ever become.

Always create new space for you.

Level Up

Boundaries mean you need to step up as a person about what you want from your life and what you want in a relationship. There are so many possibilities. Don't think along the lines of relationship, marriage, and kids. We tend to rush in and dream big, thinking this person is the one and float into that fairy tale. High levels of dopamine and other hormones are released during attraction when you first start to get to know someone, and these chemicals make us feel giddy, energetic, and euphoric. Being a bit cautious and taking things slowly will be a wise move, especially if you like this person.

If they want to see you 24/7 in the first two weeks to a month, ask yourself: does it sit right with YOU? Is my intuition in this or is it just my undies? Ha-ha. What about the idea of waiting, so that they get to know you rather than it being about noncommittal sex? They are not going to buy the cow if they can get the milk for free.

Tap into your intuition and if something is a little off and over the top, take a step back. Set the pace and set your boundaries. If it's meant to be, it will be. Don't rush. If we are lucky, we fall in love in time, but not in a week. That's the biggest red flag again: when they intensely love bomb. It is important to work on yourself and heal before entering a relationship as you tend to attract the lessons you most need to learn, and that can be hard and painful. Become whole and complete before you jump in.

An empath is so soft and beautiful, and a narcissist is lacking all of this, so they want to take it all from you then break you. The narcissist will impose all the power and control over the empath, and that's what will be taken away: the empath's beautiful soul. Just like recovering from ice addiction, so I'm told, I genuinely felt dead inside for months as I slowly rebuilt my strength.

Here is a guide of the emotional rollercoaster that you will feel when in a relationship with a narcissist. First, there is an amazing high you feel, as if you are on drugs. Then you feel confused, and you find yourself asking what's going on with this person. Next, you feel lost while feeling sad and empty. Finally, there's the blame game, where you assume it's all your fault. Then, the cycle repeats, as the narcissist delivers a little love bomb to keep you hooked.

If you feel yourself going through this type of cycle, or you are doubting and questioning yourself as to whether you should stay in the relationship or leave, it's time to really ask yourself what your worth is. If you have set strong boundaries, it's time to run and break off the relationship. This repetitive behaviour is not normal, and shouldn't be on repeat. The feelings and cycle I have described above would be my closure and time to let go and move on. You deserve better. Pink Rock!

After my birthday, the silence turned into a breakup. The silence is what gets to you, as any human who is in the dating game knows. It is just like GHOSTING! I asked the question, 'Why are we not communicating?' I didn't understand, so I messaged him. I guess from my end, I felt my puzzle wasn't complete. I had no real closure. A narcissist won't give you that. That night, we spent time together and he said, 'I love you. I don't want to hurt you.' It was a classic example of hoovering, bringing back all the trust.

He inboxed me a few months after we split, as if I was a readily available supply. With some women, there's some part of them that wants to be hoovered back. His message read as follows: 'Hi. I hope you're well. My son still asks about you.' He tried to use his son to hook me back. My response was thinking about my PINK ROCK, and creating my boundary. I gave him nothing less than nothing, which was no response.

Look at a romantic relationship between two people. We all know sex is part of a relationship. In this relationship, the empath wants to have a relationship with a soul connection. The issue is that a sexual narcissist goes into a relationship purely for sex, yet will never discuss the fact that sex and control is the only thing they want.

A narcissist will never come out and say, 'Hey, I just want a fuck. I'm going to head fuck you until I get you trapped into a trauma bond, and lock you in my room. There's no way in the world I want to do any of the beautiful things we did in the first few months. I wish you would hurry up and fall in love with me so I can spit and piss on you and bring you down to my level.' However, this is what they are thinking and it's their motive force.

GUESS WHAT? The beautiful thing is that an empath has more power than a narcissist. If you sit still in silence long enough, you can read a narcissist's map and know the cycle before you get in too deep with someone. It's actually very interesting. I can work someone's map out very early on, just by observing someone's actions on a date or in the first few weeks of starting a relationship using my superpowers and tuning into my intuition. That's why it's important to take things slowly and not risk your heart too much as you get to know someone. Over time, their true character will reveal itself.

Just because we are nice and soft hearted doesn't mean we are dumb! However, I can play dumb just a little just to test out the other side. It's a secret, so don't tell anyone. You know, flick the hair a little more, act like a Barbie doll just to get them to show their real character faster. Ha-ha!

My Five Top Tips for Dating

1. Do not go to someone's house on a first date. This is setting yourself up to say, 'I'm just here for the nookie.' Ha-ha. 'I did it for the nookie, the nookie.' That's a good song!

2. Do not tell anyone your past trauma, as it will be used against you once you are in a relationship if they are a narcissist.

3. Do not tell them your flaws, even though we all have them. They don't need to know. It is whether you can both work through them as a couple.

4. Do not tell someone you're an empath please! We are just normal strong women, because we have learnt how to set boundaries.

5. Have fun, smile, laugh, joke, and be open to learning, and who knows? You might be with the love of your life.

Something to think about is that a narcissist has great energy and appears to have higher vibrations. Why is this? Because they think they are living on a higher level than everyone. As I am an empath, I was very drawn to his energy, and it felt like a magnet to me. The energy was high for the whole six months. It was very nice to be around, and this was the biggest issue. You know when you meet a creep, or you get icky vibes? A narcissist doesn't give you that feeling.

AN EDUCATED AWARE EMPATH IS A NARCISSIST'S WORST NIGHTMARE.

 SING IT - *ELASTIC HEART* **- SIA**

 SING IT - *LOSE YOU TO LOVE ME* **- SELENA GOMEZ**

notes

Chapter Eight
healing

Healing is my favourite part. It is a process we need to take time with. Also, allow yourself more breathing space and be extra kind on your heart, especially as an empath. Healing can be the hardest part of the breakup, and so can be processing your past trauma. There will be great days and some where you may fall back down into some dark thoughts again. This is all okay and about the journey. Remember, take one day at a time.

When we accept that we need to heal, we can accept that we need time to get to the finish line. What time does is help us level up and become more balanced, more understanding, and way more aware of who we really are. It gives us a higher vibration to live with.

Healing for me has given me so much resilience, and that's why I'm so passionate about it.

I now know I had never looked within myself and healed from my past traumas. I was given two hard relationships as lessons for me to grow. This is why I found myself in the same patterns of abuse. I was acting out and attracting all I knew from a broken home. Now, I'm not blaming my parents. I love my parents, and they made me extra soft and extra strong, but believe me, broken homes have a very deep effect on a child.

A RED FLAG ISN'T A RED FLAG WHEN IT FEELS LIKE HOME

When I was eighteen and my boyfriend stabbed me, it is frightening to think about how the whole situation could've ended. His rage lasted five long minutes, and I could see it building up by the look in his eyes. What I saw in him that night, I have seen on crime scene documentaries. It was so intense, and he wasn't even in his body. As someone who loves watching crime documentaries so much, I was grateful that I have seen the look in the perpetrator and recognised this look in my then partner's eyes. It's a look of malevolence looking through you.

He would always cry when I said I was leaving him, and he would hide my keys so I couldn't drive home. Back then, I didn't believe he was a narcissist; however, he had strong traits of one. I believe he went into psychosis from being a drug addict. I forgave him. It was a young toxic love where we had a lot of good times together, and he was a big part of my life and growth.

This was my first love connection, and on every level, it felt like home to me. He would tell me he loved me so much, and he would always hug me with the most beautiful cuddles, so I felt the love that was deep in his soul. I held on to this love because I was young, with no life experience.

After the breakup, I was single until I met Ferdinand. I'd pushed a lot of good men away, because I was so scared in my subconscious mind that a good man would hurt me. I hadn't healed.

We need to forgive to heal ourselves and move forward. When I forgave, detached, and let go, that was the moment when I knew I had healed. It took two years of me being on my own to really heal.

I was still in a trauma bond for a good year after my breakup. I took time out alone to regain and grow my resilience and strength.

When I say alone, I mean alone. I didn't want to go out to see people or communicate. I felt the gym was enough socialising for me while I was healing.

They say time heals all wounds, and I'd had so much time between relationships because I didn't know that I had to heal. I never progressed with my personal development. I never had one-night stands. I never slept around to build my confidence. I knew what I had, and I did not need a man to give me confidence. However, the massive thing was that I never reflected on my own issues and healed. I just bounced along with life as I do, being cute and fluffy. Ha-ha. However, I had a wall up. I now know my pattern was my inner un-healed self, pushing men away.

Healing is your biggest blessing to get your life on track to level up and to be the best version of yourself. To bring your inner peace to any relationship, we need to forgive, detach, and let go as we step forward into the future of dating. Some days will be hard, and you know what? That's called life. The hard days are the ones that make us stronger. Use those difficult times to learn a lesson about you! Why is this day harder? What's happened that's different today? Why has it triggered me? This could be something from your past that needs healing.

Make notes on some of the pain you feel, or what the situation was that triggered you. I bet after a few times of the repetitive triggers, you'll start to see a pattern. What happened? How did I react?

Looking back, I can see I was sitting in my trauma response after the breakup with Ferds for a good year. My body was so fit yet so unhealthy on the inside, as it was living in a FREEZE response. Always looking for the murderer around every corner. This was not healthy.

Some responses to trauma can go like this:

- **FLIGHT** - When you want to get out of the situation fast.
- **FIGHT** - Can be pure self-preservation.

- **FREEZE** - When we become paused and sink into ourselves.
- **FAWN** - When we keep someone else happy, so push away the threat.

Once you understand your response and become aware of it, we find more growth. We can start working out if we are being triggered by certain events.

I guess I had to unravel my past and go through all I knew, and ask myself why. Why me? Why did I allow myself to be treated as a sex slave? Why would someone spit in my mouth and piss on me like I'm an object? Bottom line is, because I let it happen!

I was reflecting on my past trauma, my inner demons.

This experience is what I am so grateful for now, as I've found all my inner beauty. I started blossoming at thirty-seven. Now, I am stronger, smarter, and wiser. I'm proud of myself finally for saying FUCK OFF! with a little bit of feminine energy chucked in. Ha-ha.

So, how can you break the cycle of abuse? You need to go back to where you need healing. You need to look back on your life, and look at those times when you were hurt the most, or when you felt totally disillusioned. Pick the five triggers or people that hurt you the most and sit with it. It can feel so sad and uncomfortable but hey, when you are stuck in a lockdown, what better thing to do than cry and unravel your trauma to rebuild your future? Man, it's uncomfortable, sometimes we need to be uncomfortable in life or we are not growing.

I tell you, healing through lockdown was the biggest character-building exercise for me. You know why? It pulled out the trauma I didn't realise I'd had, and maybe even thoughts I'd blocked out. I'm so grateful for the dark night of the soul, and now I can appreciate how far I've come.

You can sit there and keep asking, why me? Why? Why? Why? Or, you can work on understanding why. Take on the challenge and do the hard yards. We are such creatures of passing the blame and saying it's someone else's fault. What happens to you is a reflection of what you think of yourself, and this can be subconsciously as well. A narcissist is just a child un-healed. They just won't ever look at themselves, because they are perfect in their eyes. This is where an empath has the upper hand.

Passing the blame is not going to help you heal. It's just going to make you hold onto the anger, when your best purpose is to release it.

We look at break ups like falling over, thinking if I just get up and rub the dirt off,

I'll be okay to move on. A lot of people go searching for new love to fulfill that empty part in their heart, when the love they need to find is within THEMSELVES and we all need to learn to love ourselves! A new love won't heal you. You just will be taking the problems or issues you haven't dealt with into the next relationship, and who wants that?

My number one rule of a no-go zone in dating is when the new person speaks about the ex and the problems they had. Why? Because they haven't detached from that person, which means they haven't healed and to me, that means you are coming in second place, and who wants to talk about their exes? NO, THANK YOU! Here is where I'll just pass my potential new partner my book. Ha-ha, just kidding.

Wait for the Bones to Heal

Look at someone with broken bones who has been in a car accident. They take time to heal, and they don't just get up and start walking or go skydiving. It takes time for them to get their strength back emotionally, mentally, and physically.

Coming out of an abusive relationship is the same. For some, especially when coming out of a relationship with a narcissist, it is so hard, because you won't get closure. They keep all the doors open, in case they run out of their supply. Your discard and your devaluation are your signal to end it and get closure. Someone continually pushing or trampling over your boundaries is another sign. The way they treat you is your signal for closure. PINK ROCK them to heal. Bring back your beautiful soul into the sunlight and shine.

You might have 'broken bones' that need time to heal, and people may not understand you. Remember that it's okay for you to take more time than others to get over what has happened. Everyone is different and unique. Your heart is obviously soft and real.

Here's a question though. Does this happen too often? Have you broken out of your past cycle of abuse? If you keep being presented with the same situations, behaviours, or scenarios, you haven't healed. It's your trial. What does this mean? Have you set a boundary?

It's important to realise that you are still healing, and could be heading back into the wrong relationships because you don't know who you are, or you don't know how to break out of the cycle of repeating past patterns of behaviour. Grabbing onto any form of love because you haven't learnt your WORTH isn't going to be the best for you. Doing what you've always done will lead you to where you have always been. Who wants that?

I'm so grateful for the dark night of the soul, and now I can appreciate how far I've come.

Chapter Eight: Healing

Are you following the same footsteps from your past because it's common ground that feels familiar and it's all you know?

Here is the really cool news. You can retrain your brain and thoughts to bring about a nicer future and get what you deserve. You must BELIEVE and BE UNAPOLOGETICALLY YOU! My big sister Vikki taught me that. xx

Ask

Talk to yourself better. Talk about your day more positively. We bring into our life what we think, so if we think negative thoughts, we will get negative results - how powerful! So, if you want to heal, take the time to ASK! 'Heavenly Father, I need help in healing. Please help release all bad energy and bad thoughts about me so I can bring forward my inner peace. Help me become a stronger version of myself. Help me get to the place of resilience so I know my healing is at its end, and help keep all unwanted people away from me while I'm doing so.'

Now you have a little prayer to help you every day.

When we look at healing, we are all unique and we may use different ways to heal. You might find a mountain path to walk on and unleash your pain, or you might like to start a new hobby that has always interested you, or you could set a new goal to help yourself move forward. When you are healing, it's a very good time to reflect and do mirror work. Ask yourself the hard questions like, 'Am I being the best version of myself?' or 'Who would want to date me?'

Maybe seek out a therapist if you need to. The right person can help you peel back those layers, and give you practical help to work your way through why you are where you are at. Sometimes, it takes effort to find the person that you feel will work the best with you. Talking to a distant ear is sometimes the best medicine.

As an empath, we feel vibrations from the top half of ourselves, feel the energy around us making sure we are safe and the people around us are safe. We don't necessarily feel our own vibrations. The cool thing I've noticed after my healing and spiritual awakening is that now I can feel my own vibrations, energy, and anything that may trigger me to put myself first.

I spent a few years understanding and learning about myself. I've experienced so much growth, and I now love myself from my ugly toes to my beautiful fat heart and my cute as fuck face. Ha-ha. How funny are my photos when I point my toes like a ballerina. When I point my toes is how you know I'm over concentrating. I do it writing also. Ha-ha.

I know I'm not perfect, and like everyone, I have faults but I'm doing my best to understand them and become a better version of myself. I'm focusing on my breathing work more, and using one day a week on my own in the sun as a part of my personal therapy and recharge day.

I like to think of myself as a pink rose with a few spikes and a sprinkling of spice, because I am a little bit of both. I spend time getting to know myself and valuing my worth. I mean, I didn't even date and I closed myself off as I knew I had to date myself and love myself and hey, I discovered that I'm pretty bloody cool. I am so fun to hang out with. I sing. I laugh. I eat. I cook for myself. I love group fitness and staying fit, and I love diving in the ocean which I do every day. When people ask why my face is so clear, I say dive in the ocean, and when you do, your mind becomes clearer too. I love watching Disney films or crime investigations on my own as well. Ha-ha. Talk about yin and yang.

The Easy Road to Fame

A few years before my spiritual awakening, I applied to go on Married at First Sight two years in a row, and the year before that, I auditioned for The Bachelor. I made it to the final rounds every time. One day, on the way to the set of Married at First Sight, I found another playing card, which was a message for me. Looking back, I know that this was a sign for me to stop and take stock of what was happening. At the time, I was a bit upset about getting so close to finding love and fame, yet not making it to the very end. After all, lots of people have told me that I could become famous, as I exude that energy.

On reflection, I hadn't healed, and I was trying to be someone that I wasn't supposed to be. Once I had gone through the healing process, I realised that being on the shows and finding love that way wasn't my destiny. I needed to work hard to get to my new destination, and writing this book was me doing the hard yards and healing. When life doesn't go your way and you're asking 'Why me? Why me?', understand that perhaps what you wanted wasn't meant for you and you are being asked to take a different direction.

Writing was a big part of my healing. I wrote The Golden Mask years back while I was going through the motions of the breakup with the narcissist, trying to unravel and understand his sick mind. I guess it was more of my self-help book at the time; however, my intuition always pulled me back to my writing and using the golden mask. I just wasn't sure how I was going to bring it to life. I hadn't even read the Golden Mask for a few years, as I had let it all go and didn't want to reread it again.

Chapter Eight: Healing

A clairvoyant read my cards through the first lockdown. She said, 'Wow. You know things. You have a very high intuition of vibrations. You love writing and you need to write.' Well, yeah, this is how the path that led me to the cover became a reality. She also told me to ask for more help, so I did.

I always endeavour to be grateful and present in everything that I do. This is a great way to heal. If we are thinking of our past, it can make us sad that it's passed. If we think of our future, it makes us anxious of what's to come. Be present. My book is setting me up for my future self, but I've enjoyed being so present in my writing.

Ask yourself what you are grateful for, and keep a notebook of these thoughts with the ones that make you sad. Things should start to feel happier as the months move on and you heal.

You can also stand in the shower and yell out your pain if that works best. I didn't try this one. I had to let yelling be released from my mind and soul through writing, and here it is. Ha-ha.

Once you detach from your traumas, you are unstoppable, and you will notice the shift in your relationships and vibrations. Be extra kind with your heart and soul, and remember it wasn't your fault. You were manipulated and ended up in this mess. Remember, the narcissist is an expert in one area and one area only, and that is manipulation. It definitely isn't sex; however, they think they are experts at it.

If you can think of five people or moments where you have been hurt, write them a letter, and get your pain out. You don't have to send them the letter. Just think of it as a way of releasing your pain and anger. What you have written down on the paper is your key to knowing what area you need to start to heal from. Get all your pain out and feel every emotion. If it's triggering you, you have found your starting point. A therapist might be able to help you with this. You need to go back, rebuild yourself and heal. Once you've called them every fucking name under the sun, you need to detach and forgive to move forward.

Remember that forgiving someone doesn't mean that you are okay with what someone has done to you. It means that you are no longer willing to carry around the pain that they inflicted on you. This clearing will enable you to open your heart and soul up, and let all your walls down. You'll be free of your past, become present in the moment, and ready for your future.

Letter to the Narc

DEAR FERDINAND,

I want to thank you for pushing me to believe in myself. I want to thank you for letting me see all my beautiful magic in my heart and soul. Most of all, YOU HELPED ME CHANGE MY PATH. 'I'm going this way, while YOU SIT IN THE TRENCHES!!

(He always said that to me.)

You always said I was the happiest person you've met. Hence why you needed to pull me down to your level. So, you can only imagine how happy I am now. You took six months of my life that turned into a year and a half from you sucking my soul dry. I feel sorry for you to be that low, and so addicted to sex to do what you did to two and probably more innocent women. I also want you to know I've enjoyed un-jumbling you like my very own crime scene, and you know how much I love crime mysteries, so thank you!

PS - I am strong, aren't I!

SING IT - *I DID IT MY WAY* **- FRANK SINATRA**

HOW DO YOU KNOW IF YOU ARE HEALING?

YOU DON'T BLAME YOURSELF.

YOU ARE BREAKING OLD PATTERNS.

YOU SPEAK UP FOR YOURSELF WITHOUT WORRYING what others might think.

YOU SET BOUNDARIES about how you want to be treated and respected.

YOU REALISE IT'S SAFE TO BE YOU.

YOU RECOGNISE AND DISMANTLE TRIGGERS.

YOU ARE NOT ASHAMED OF ASKING FOR HELP.

PINK ROCK THEM FOR YOUR HEART.

The Next Steps

With your pages of sadness and extra pages of happiness, write your own personal journal to reflect on how far you've come and help you destress. Remember that taking and using baby steps consistently leads to massive achievements. Be proud of yourself. For example, when I was writing this book, I set myself up with an intention to write for fifty minutes to an hour every day, just as if I am doing a workout. This was my way of using baby steps to move me towards my goal. If I had not been disciplined and stuck to my baby steps, I would have never written this book.

Fun

Make sure you remember to play like a kid, and don't get trapped in the thoughts, 'I'm healing, so I can't have fun.' We need to unleash our silly energy and play more. How do we have fun?

Do something that will bring joy and fun to every level of you. Get off your phone and turn off the TV! Being creative is what I love, and music is my thing. It's a feeling that goes through my soul. It can change my mood and ease my mind on any level of emotion. Dance classes and pole dancing would be so much fun, but I think I'll stick to my spin bike.

Being fit and well is a way of being that you cannot beat. Feeling good and looking good is only going to make you strong! Let's go!

Train your mind. Find a new passion or a new purpose and tell yourself daily: 'I am strong. I am beautiful. I am funny, and I am happy and healthy.' Say it with power and with a positive mindset. Affirmations can be written on notes and placed around your living area where you will see them often, thus helping train your mind and thoughts into a better mindset.

I am very blessed to be a fitness instructor. RPM is my happy place, because of the music and adrenaline that gets released in my body. My RPM classes helped me heal. I'm so grateful to anyone who has been in my classes in Bondi and Market St Fitness First, as you have helped me as much as I hope I've helped you. Alice, Hilary, Sona, Tom, and my boy Harry, THANK YOU! It helped me feel strong and in control of my life, even though track six made a few of us cry. Ha-ha. That's the best part of music and emotions. You feel.

Think of and plan a new path, and detach from the old past. Break RULES. We are all so blinded and misguided in life by rules. For example, have a nine to five job, own a house, and get married. I say fuck the rules, break them, and follow your own path. Watch what happens as you become a strong mother fucker who can't be fucked with.

Do one thing for me. Shut your eyes. Look at your eight-year-old self. Give her a hug, and tell her you will make her proud and safe. Give that little girl what she needs. Protect yourself the way you wanted your eight-year-old self to be protected. Heal for her.

Now, look at the eighty-year-old you! Make that person so happy to the point where if they are on their own, they can laugh and smile about the life you gave them. You have healed and lived.

SING IT - *EASY ON ME* - ADELE

SING IT - *BREATHE IN NOW* - GEORGE

Chapter Eight: Healing

notes

Chapter Nine

your intuition is your biggest gift

Wow! Where do I even begin with intuition? As an empath, we have a super brain; however, it only works when you use your intuition and a boundary together.

What is intuition? It's a sign from your gut. It never lies! Did you know that your gut is your second brain and far more powerful? You know when you get butterflies or that sick feeling when you see someone who has upset you? There is this feeling that travels all the way up to your heart and head. It's a feeling that travels to your mind to give you a message that's needed. Mia Steiber describes intuition as an inner knowing. It's a delicate gentle feeling, asking us to notice something that isn't right or needs our attention. It's a feeling from your gut where you instinctively know that something you are doing is either right or wrong. Sometimes, when you ignore it, your intuition will keep coming back in. I always think of it like a message from my angel guiding me, and I think 'okay, okay, I didn't listen very well.' Ha-ha. I do now! Intuition for me is a calm feeling that comes from my core to protect me and guide me. I know it will never lie to me. It's like an inner knowing or an inner voice trying to speak to you.

Intuition can happen in a heartbeat and disappear, so if you get a thought, maybe write it down so you don't forget it. I know I can wake up at 3 am with a very strong feeling from my intuition. Sometimes, my intuition is the first thing that speaks to me, and it's where a lot of creative people get their best ideas.

I feel we all need to use our intuition more, change directions more, take more chances. I genuinely believe you become stronger and build more resilience by doing so.

If we look at life as a kid, you get handed everything. We are given food, a pen, and paper at school, and told what sport to play. There are so many rules. We often don't have an understanding about our intuition until we are older enough to understand it.

So, what happens? We continue waiting for things to be handed to us! We apply for jobs we think we want or jobs to get us money. Is this really what you are passionate about? If so, good for you. If not, use some intuition and make life a little challenging.

Before writing this book during the lockdowns, I felt like I was in a dark tunnel, and something was pulling me through it.

When you let your intuition guide you, you can feel like a mixture of emotions. It's a little scary, a little new, and it's exciting, with a little bit of the unknown thrown in. I felt like I kind of wanted to put my head in the dark tunnel then pull away from it, but then something soft was pulling me back in. Once I started walking, following the footsteps of my intuition, this beautiful light started shining, leading the way I needed to be going. Then, it became a trip into this amazing garden of extra beautiful flowers, full of possibilities. My intuition was so powerful and magical. I could feel more creativity coming in and empowering me, and I wanted to use it. If I didn't follow my intuition, you wouldn't be reading my story today.

We put roadblocks up and tell ourselves negative stories and doubt ourselves, asking questions like what if it doesn't work? What if my intuition pulls me somewhere wrong? It's natural to feel that uncertainty, but if you don't try, you will never find out and you will stay in that place of being stuck.

Deep down, there will be a voice that questions you and asks you if this is what makes you happy. Are you loving your job? Is this what you want for the rest of your life? This is why most people get stuck in a nine to five job they hate. They don't try to tap into their intuition and inner guidance. They don't listen and ignore it.

And why is this? I genuinely believe because it's all we know we have been programmed from a young age, basically like living zombies who march and do as we are told.

An example of a story and a roadblock to me tapping into and using my intuition was when my head said, 'I need to stay in my job because I need money. I need to live.' My head wanted to keep me safe and financially secure, and for a long time, the protection of a stable income that kept me in Bondi.

My heart asked, 'How will I leave my job as a group fitness instructor?' After all, my clients had become more like family, and I felt like I was a leader of our little fitness community. I was thinking of all the lovely people I formed friendly relationships with and cherished. We had shared so much love and laughs together over time through my classes. By leaving this job that I loved and by leaving all the people that I was helping, I really felt like I was letting a lot of people down. They were like my second family, and I didn't want to upset them.

My intuition said, 'This is about you, your dream, and your purpose. Listen and follow your magic.'

It's about taking that step of faith within you. Watch all the miraculous doors open, and the beautiful flower fields grow more and more as your life streams in new directions. Dance a little more. Dive a little more, and smile brighter. You never know what might happen!

Looking at the positive side of the last few years, if this pandemic never happened, this version of who I am right now would never exist. I quit two jobs to get myself where I am now. In the end, I listened to my intuition and took a giant leap of faith to complete this book. If I hadn't listened, I wouldn't have been able to create my new destiny, and be who and where I am now.

How You Can Tap into Your Intuition

I think it's all about listening to your inner voice, or as some people like to call it, your higher self. People with strong intuition are very connected to their spirit.

To feel it or tap into it, try to find somewhere quiet and alone where you can be at peace, breathe, and listen to your thoughts. If there is a situation you need guidance on, trust a little more and focus on that area. Your intuition will come to you. Maybe not then and there, but a message will come through if you believe. Ask some questions about what you want to bring into your future five years and ten years from now. Your mind might start preparing you for a new path, and this is your intuition directing you.

Be in the moment. Be present and still your mind from the stories and doubts you are telling yourself, or that other people have told you. This is where meditation can help too as it quietens your mind, slows you down, and clears the channels that communicate with you.

I would always start with baby steps. One day, you might ask the Universe for guidance. Speak from your heart and ask the questions you need answered whether it be about work, a relationship, dating, or even moving onto a new career path.

How to move forward in your life? LEVEL UP! Focus on that one thing you desire. The more you speak, the easier it becomes and the clearer the answers. As your intuition guides you towards your new reality, you will get epiphanies or little signs to follow. You need to take that leap of faith. Jump!

Believe! Believe in you. No one is coming for you! No one is going to do the work for you. You need to trust yourself. When you get on a plane or a ship, you trust the people that control the vehicle and you don't even know who they are, so start trusting yourself.

Write things down you want answered. Manifest, be still with yourself and be present.

You will start getting signs, so be alert and open. Lean into that sign

more and if it feels a little scary, that's exciting! Learn more. Remember to follow that tunnel to the pink flower fields.

For me, praying hasn't come easy. I didn't grow up in a religious family, and I don't go to church. Sometimes, I will listen to a few prayers on TikTok to help me calm my soul and ask for guidance.

The more I worked on myself becoming still, the more still I became, and the more I was able to pray. Now, I can easily say a prayer, and I feel I am on my right path by following my intuition.

I love acting and doing TikTok, and I've always wanted to be in an Aldi ad. Ha-ha. Having trust in my future and trust in myself is helping me step into what might come in my life without worrying about the what ifs. I am leaning into that tunnel, and it feels so exciting. I need to say it: 'ALDI. GOOD DIFFERENT!' My motto for me as a person is just like the ad: good different.

Something that I have learned about myself is that I can't operate from three places at once. In the past, I tended to give all my energy away to other people. Looking back, this was why I needed to step back from teaching and my other job. I had to put myself first, and this was the way I could move forward and follow my intuition. I began to set some strong boundaries, and I knew I had to put my head and my heart aside.

These actions all came from a place of calm. When you allow your intuition and the Universe will guide you, you start to block any shit paths that you're on. That's the magic of intuition. Your intuition never lies. Everyone has something magical within them. It comes down to whether you are strong enough to level up and use the power of your intuition that's trying to protect you and make you fly.

Red Flags

On so many occasions, even from the second week with little Ferds, I had red flag moments. My gut was pulling at me, tapping at me, and telling me his behaviour wasn't normal. Thinking back, it was the over intense love bombing, the deep loving conversations in the beginning, and the over obsessed touching which had me wondering.

The main red flag was the sex. Being addicted to PORN is an absolute deal breaker for me!

The people who are addicted to porn are the most depressed. It honestly kills their souls. Why would I ignore that? He said he will never use me for sex like other men whilst grabbing my face, looking into my soul and creating a trauma bond whilst planning on doing the complete opposite. The obsessions and weird behaviour were pulling at my core, telling me to wake the fuck up! My intuition kicked in when he started pacing the floor, because it was a behaviour pattern I've never witnessed before.

A very nervous lying energy.

We need to really think more when we are in these situations that are making us feel uneasy or unsure. Otherwise, the tunnel will lead in the opposite direction, away from the pink flower fields towards a darker tunnel, leaving you feeling sad and empty as if you have no soul left. I felt like he had sucked my soul, body, and mind dry.

Listen to that red flag feeling, and don't be afraid to run. It can come out of the blue. Like a random dream almost, and you are thinking, 'Why now?' It's like your angel is yelling at you to wake the fuck up, if angels spoke like that. Ha-ha. It's your protection, so make sure you listen.

I can get very quiet sometimes in conversations or situations as my intuition communicates with me. As an empath, I feel my intuition on a higher level. It doesn't come from a place of judgement, anger, or sadness. It's just a feeling or answer I get in my gut sometimes. It's like I can finish someone's sentence, or I've listened to what they are telling me in double time. Ha-ha. I know if someone is lying. I don't concentrate but the truth is, it's because I'm ahead of what we are talking about, and I do get bored. Ha-ha. Whoops!

The Big Three

I felt like I was walking around with three strong parts of me being pulled in three different directions. Thoughts were coming in from my head, my heart, and my intuition, and that's where the confusion came in for me as well as not knowing the language at the time.

I remember when I was thirty-three, I was at the age where I was ready to meet someone and settle down. I had my mum on my back about meeting someone - you know, as mothers do. My **head** took over, and I thought being able to take a man to family gatherings would make my mum happy and I thought it meant that I was whole and complete. Basically, I thought I needed to have someone to be happy. When happiness comes from within.

My main driving thoughts were that I needed to settle down, and I needed to be in a relationship. This was the man people told me to go after: someone different,

Dance a little more. Dive a little more, and smile brighter. You never know what might happen!

the gentleman. My **heart** was sending me messages, like 'I love this man's energy. We get along very well, and we have a lot in common.' It felt fun and interesting. The love chemical dopamine was working well.

Your intuition is your biggest gift. It knows. At the beginning of this relationship, my **intuition** was pulling me back. It felt like I was standing up, trying to grab this beautiful cake. I was leaning in to grab it at the bakery, and this angel was pulling my arm, telling me it was poison. I had both arms reaching out. When I grabbed the cake, my angel sat staring at me with her arms crossed, saying something like, 'I did try and stop you, but you love food too much.' Ha-ha. Then she sprinkled fairy dust on my head, trying to wake me up. Sadly for me, I didn't listen and kept reaching out for more cake. We all know how it feels when we eat too much cake!

WTF? A Card?

I believe my pop is my biggest guardian angel. When he was alive, we were close. He passed away when I was twenty-seven and sadly, I was in England at the time. I never got to say goodbye, but I feel he is by my side. His signs are so intense, to the point where he throws cards under my feet when I'm in shit situations. I have been finding playing cards randomly on the ground since he passed. I've found at least sixteen cards so far.

When he died, I asked him to tell me when I'd met the love of my life. I've always asked him for guidance, and these cards came down when I was in challenging situations. The one I remember most was when I was walking to work in the pissing down rain from Ferdinand's place. I found a card which I picked up, and I remember the feeling in my gut (intuition) asking me what the hell I was doing.

Another funny instance was a little card I found on a date. I was at the Bucket List in Bondi, and I needed a toilet break. The card was on the bathroom floor. I had a little laugh to myself, and sent a Snapchat to my sisters saying, 'On a date. Found this. Pop said he has a small willy.' Ha-ha. They laughed.

I believe he was telling me to fall in love with myself, find myself, and love me, and stop being so fluffy. The cards turned up in moments when I needed a message and guidance, and the funny thing was that I have never found them since I've fallen in love with me! I find the rainbow instead.

This was my moment when I knew I was done. My relationship with Ferdinand was finished. I went to Ferd's place, as I hadn't seen him for a week, and he had his son that weekend. I felt I was already being pushed out the door by that stage. Yes, I understand him feeling exhausted after having a child all weekend, but he didn't even greet me with a hello. He was laying in his bed with his head in his phone. He said to me, 'I've been busy. I deserve some down time.' Well yeah, obviously, I thought, but could he get off his phone to greet me and have a normal conversation? He stayed in bed watching Ultimate Fighting Championship (UFC). I knew for me, this was me done.

Once he was finished watching his fight, his words were, 'Come upstairs', which meant come upstairs for sex. He sprinted up the stairs in a flash, without even having a conversation with me. That was when I stood up and said, 'I am done with this shit. I know my worth and who I am. You are just a fake piece of demanding work!'

Little did I know that my intuition had kicked in! At that time, I couldn't explain the shift of strength that occurred in me. When you step back and look in, it's crazy how wonderful your body is at trying to guide you and protect you at the same time.

So, when I look back at life, this is what I see.

I see rules that have been brainwashed into us.

Go to school. Have lunch at a given time. Go to work and have dinner at 6pm. Have a family. Have kids. Tick the boxes and then that's life, but what if that's not for you?

Follow your intuition. I had always been in trouble at school because I couldn't follow rules. I've never been able to concentrate during school, and I still struggle with concentration when participating in small talk. I was caught up with all the rules, telling me to do this and do that. I've always had a different way of thinking, and I guess I could be dyslexic. I see life as a series of puzzles and patterns. Being creative from a younger age and never being able to express it, as school is all about - 1+1 = 3. We all know that. Ha-ha! How boring!

Being an empath is very strong in me. I like to work things out by observing people. I can sit and watch someone, and in a few hours, I can tell them more things about themselves than they would have known. I could even give them a free counselling session. Ha-ha!

I can explain things to people to help them understand from a different point of view or perspective. This, I guess, comes from following my own intuition. It has helped me collect so much awareness in my life that I am then able to put into words for someone to understand. I feel grateful that I can help a person see a situation with a sense of clarity.

If you keep following society's rules and expectations, you might feel depressed or sad if that's not sitting well with you. So, do what makes you happy. Divide your brain into four squares: 1. Doing what you've been told, 2. What you have learnt, 3. What you are going to do, and most importantly, 4. WHAT DO YOU WANT?

Knowing what you want is about digging deep within yourself. You need to sit and ask for help and guidance, and be receptive. You will get answers. My book is living proof. For someone who is unable to concentrate for long periods of time, not a good speller, and for someone who was kicked out of most of my classes at school, I think I have done alright. From every failing point in my life, I've turned it all around. For example, I've written a book and am starting a second book for children. All I've done is follow my intuition, and YOU CAN TOO!

Follow the yellow brick road. My intuition made me write this book!

That was going to be the title, but my intuition said otherwise.

SING IT - *CUZ I CAN* - PINK

Chapter Nine: Your Intuition Is Your Biggest Gift

notes

Chapter Ten

the power of not giving a fuck

The Path that Led Me to the Cover

I always get told that I am brave and confident in ways other people don't dare to be. I've never really looked at myself as having those character traits. I am just me. I talk to rich people the same way I do to the less fortunate, and I would never look down on someone who has less than me or more than me.

I could put the worst TikTok up and laugh my ass off at myself, and I couldn't care less if someone said something nasty about it. I couldn't give a fuck. To me, that's just their own insecurity coming out. I never write hateful comments on anyone's post. If it doesn't resonate with me, I'll just scroll past. That's one big thing that's wrong with the world. There seems to be so many nasty comments out there, and yet those commenting have no idea what that person has been through in their life or even that day! My advice is to keep your mouth shut! Remember what you put out in this world comes back to you, so be mindful.

I understand my sense of humour is a little different but hey, not everyone wants a mango. Some people want grapes. Ha-ha.

Don't let other people get to you. I keep my circle of friends small and loyal. I have so many amazing people in my life, but I don't have thousands. I like real people who I love and trust. I'm not fake, and can't deal with the fake shit that goes on in this life. It makes me sad, so I stay away from it. PINK ROCK!

I find it harder to fit in with the outside world after going through my spiritual awakening. Being awake has made me remove myself from social scenes, and massive crowds make me anxious as I collect too much energy then leave really drained. I'd rather spend time in the sun holding pretty flowers. Ha-ha.

MY FAMILY ARE FUNNY AF. We are very silly people who love to laugh, and we don't give many fucks. If we want to dress up and go out, great. Otherwise it's PJs and silly laughs on the floor at home. Sometimes, mum's flat on the floor laughing.

We don't have a lot of money or valuables, but one thing we have that is more important is love. There is so much love in my family, and I'm so grateful as this is where my morals and respect has come from. All we need is love.

Chapter Ten: The Power Of Not Giving A Fuck

'Inspirational' Quotes from My Family

Mum - *'You were beautiful even when you were fat.'*

My mummy lost her mum and dad at a young age.

Me to my mum - *'I'm so proud of you. You are my hero. I love you.'*

Dad - *'You can't write a book. You don't even know how to spell cat.'*

My dad has been clear of throat cancer for five years now. He is my strength.

Rachel - *'You are smarter than I thought.'*

She is my big sister who has been clean from ice for four years, and is killing it at life. She has guns of steel and is my best friend.

Stacey - *'You have a fat heart and ugly feet.'*

Stacey is my little sister who is a beautiful mummy of my two little favourite people. I've loved watching you 'GLOW UP.'

'Lillian, you are my best friend,' from the movie Bridesmaids. Ha-ha.

Finally, there's my little brother Mathew whose vocabulary seems to consist of *'What? What do you want me to say?'* You have a very incredible gift that not many people have and its magic. I hope you realise how talented you are when you bring your music to life. You only have one life, so reach high and take that guitar by its strings. I'm proud of you!

My favourite cousin Az - *'You are so ugly.'*

He is my big pain in the arse cousin, but he is like a big brother. You know what? I have nothing nice to say to you!

This is your life.
Don't let people get to you.

I find I can get judged easily on my appearance or the fact I lived in Bondi. 'Oh, typical Bondi girl. Big tits, nice body, and probably stuck up.'

I love the fact that that statement is so far from the truth. The best line I've heard is, 'Oh. You must go for the Roosters. Ha-ha.' My response was, 'No, I don't. I actually go for Parramatta.' Then they look at me like a stunned fish.

Sometimes people are in shock if I say hello to them. It's as if they are thinking 'Why would I be nice?' Ha-ha. I'm the weird girl who says hello at the most random of times.

Here's the thing. I've been judged my whole life. At school, kids would tease me and say that I smelt yukky because I swam every morning in a chlorinated pool. This is where my story stems from. I now get called crazy, weird, a headcase, not well in the head, or left of field. However, that's fair because my TikTok presence is all of that. That's my 25% extroverted creative self who loves to perform and entertain. I do think left of field and my mind doesn't stop wanting to create. When I sit still and watch people, I gather so much information. I have a photographic memory. This is how I get into so many characters on my TikTok. Ha-ha. I watch and I feel - something Ferdinand didn't think about when he told me he needed to be careful with what he said around me.

I've enjoyed writing my story, and consider it a great personal accomplishment. I'm proud of myself. I created it, from the cover to the photos with visuals, songs, words, and everything else in between. I loved adding the pretty dresses for each chapter for all my visual readers. It's all those pieces of the book that makes my brain happy. No one has ever said to me, 'Oh! Hey. You're very intelligent. Why is that? I think it is because people are so fast to judge on physical appearance alone. People like to bring you down. Like how many talents can one have? Ha-ha. Well, you cannot judge a book by its cover. Like a narcissist who presents a good image to the outside world, no one knows what they are really like, and they do not know what is happening behind closed doors.

I'm a very calm person. I just turn on a show at the click of a switch, like Ferdinand the bull. He puts on a show for the outside world, and my stage is TikTok and group fitness.

I DONT GIVE A FUCK WHAT PEOPLE THINK.

Run at Me
Once in a conversation with a guy, we were speaking about intuition and how I know what I know. His response was, 'I don't think you know things.' He loved

bringing me down. I genuinely couldn't respond. My mind just thinks, 'You are rude' Comments like that make me push myself. More to the point, that one sentence is what pushed me to write my story. If I'm having a hard day and yes, I am human. I do have sad days and I sometimes hear his words, 'I don't think you know things.' Then I laugh and write a little more, because I use those moments as my fuel.

So, if you want to wear that weird bright pink dress with bright pink shoes and carry that green clutch that doesn't match your bright yellow nails, make sure you put some bright lipstick on with it and send me a photo. I'll credit it all over my TikTok with love.

This is your life. Don't let people get to you.

I'm never going to judge anyone. I love that we are all different, so why would we judge one another when we have never walked a day in their shoes?

One of my favourite pastimes is walking around the city watching people, or sitting on the train and listening to conversations. I find people fascinating. Once, there was the guy playing his music with no teeth, having the best day of his life out the front of Woolworths. He didn't care about the millions of dollars. He was just trying to get a chocolate bar as someone walked past.

Girls are like flowers; we are all different and beautiful in our own way. You never look at a flower and say, 'Well that's a bloody ugly flower.' I think I'm a pink rose. Ha-ha. I have a few thorns on my stem, but once you get to my heart, I'm a beautiful soft pink rose. I don't want to be the perfect red one.

My beautiful best friend is the tallest, most beautiful white stemmed rose I've ever seen. Her legs are beautiful and long, while her heart is pure and white and there isn't anything more perfect than a pretty, white rose. Never above anyone and never below anyone. She is six foot one, so maybe a little higher than me, but she is always by my side or I'm probably by hers more.

Attitude is everything, and being positive will have enormous benefits to you throughout your day. Every morning, you wake up, pull your shoulders back, hold your head up high, and power stance at that door. Tell yourself, 'I've got this. I'm coming into my day like a boss, and I don't give a fuck!' Remember that you can set strong boundaries, and other peoples' judgements are their stuff and not yours.

People tell me that I am so beautiful and that I get away with everything. You know what? It's because I have a carefree attitude. It has nothing to do with my looks and believe me, I was worse with my attitude when I was young and chubby. Ha-ha. I used to dance on the table at school, and everyone used to laugh at me because they thought I was hilarious. I've never changed. You know what has? People's perception of me.

 SING IT - *A COVER IS NOT THE BOOK* **- MARY POPPINS (one of my favourite movies)**

I've never changed. You know what has? People's perceptions of me.

Chapter Ten: The Power Of Not Giving A Fuck

notes

Harper Vera-Lee

My Purpose, My First True Love

You are strong my girl. You are beautiful. You are kind and you have a very strong intuition. It's a gift that not all humans are blessed to have. You are an empath. You love deeply and you care deeply. You need to protect your heart the way you protect your baby dolls, the whole forty-five of them. Ha-ha. I see your magic and I can feel your magic.

You need to understand the world is a big hard place for soft souls. It's important for you to find your worth, your purpose, and your strength. Never let anyone stand in your way. Your intuition will guide you through life.

Level up!!! and find the power of the word NO. If you need to use it, say no, and kick them in the ball sack, the way you kick in karate.

YOU HAVE SUPERPOWERS.

People will come and go. They will be a lesson or a blessing. Understand that the Universe is teaching you to stand tall, and it will keep throwing the same mistakes at you until you learn to be stronger than that mistake. It's your lesson.

Follow your magical path to the pink flower garden. You, my angel, will fall but you will get back up! Every single time, dust off your knees and run at the world like your aunty. I LOVE YOU!

My story is for any mother, auntie, or single father who has a magical little girl in their life.

Take the time to get to know her. Put down your phone and spend quality time with her. Her presence in your life is a gift. Understand her, and let her dream her dreams and follow her path. Teach her to protect herself when she is at an age to date.

Narcissistic abuse was never taught to me in my past. I had never even heard of the term, and couldn't understand how someone could be so clever and manipulative, yet so low to do such things to an innocent girl. A girl who just loves to love, who trusted, and wanted a family. My story is to help you educate her to save her going through what I went through.

 SING IT - *FIGHT SONG* **- RACHEL PLATTEN**

Love Harper

Chapter Eleven

never judge unless you've walked someone's path

The Path that Led Me to the Cover

My story started here. I grew up in a country town called Bomaderry. Being chubby as a kid affected me more than I realised. There are only so many times a child can be called fat without it really making them sad, silent, and reserved.

My mum and dad split when I was twelve. From there, I moved to different homes. Moving around like we did was very unsettling for a child to take on board. When I went through the dark night of the soul, my flashbacks consisted of screams, yelling, and negative words used towards me.

In high school, I floated around many groups, probably just carrying on with nonsense. I was still chubby then, and I remember this boy who chucked a stick at me and said, 'Sucked in fatty' as it hit me. My beautiful friends would always say, 'Kim, you have a cute face.' I'd always say 'Well, when you are young, you are skinny and when you are old, you are fat, so I'll be skinny'. Ha-ha. Who says that at sixteen?

Well yeah, I guess my manifesting and kindness did come back to me. I was never a bitchy person as it's not in my nature, and never will be.

When I was at school, I never had a boy ask me out or think of me as pretty. My friends always picked up 'that cute guy' at a party. I was always reserved, because I was a tom boy and chubby. I never had confidence. I guess I told myself I didn't deserve love because I was fat. No one picked me. I kind of told myself 'A STORY', and that story was that I didn't deserve love. Now, I DO DESERVE LOVE AND I HAVE SO MUCH LOVE TO GIVE to the right people. I now know my fucking worth and the amount of love I deserve! We all tend to have 'a story.'

I was a state swimmer from the young age of eight until I was sixteen. I'm very grateful to my mum for keeping me in swimming as it's helped me with having structure in my life, but swimming wasn't my thing. I wasn't really interested in winning or making swimming my life, so I quit at the age of sixteen. I told my coach, 'I'm going to be a drummer'. HA-HA.

I put on a lot of weight, and I guess being a little intuitive, I started thinking about how I could be skinny. I wanted boys to notice me. What could I do? I was fat and ugly, so at age seventeen, I walked into the Bomaderry Fitness Centre and got my first membership. I started group fitness, and I used to stand down the back so no one could see me. I was fat, had chafe between my thighs, and I couldn't even lunge. I was so embarrassed, but instead of giving up, I would do squats in the lunge track during body pump.

For me, it was the music that pulled me into the group fitness studio. I started reading about diets in magazines, and I started buying women's health magazines to learn more. I was seventy-eight kilos at the time, and I remember sitting in my room saying little prayers and doing my best to manifest the outcome I wanted. Even if I didn't grow up in a church home, my spirit was very strong. I'd study magazines, and I had lots of surfing girl photos on my wall for inspiration alongside JUSTIN TAYLOR THOMAS. HA-HA.

Then I started losing weight, and I became addicted to group fitness. I loved it. I trained seven days a week, and even did the Saturday morning body combat classes when I was hungover. I was eighteen.

I started getting noticed by men out in clubs. Guys would always call me young Tara Reid, and I felt special for the first time in my life. I got my first boyfriend when I was eighteen. For me, I only wanted that one love. He took something from me that I didn't want any other man to have. I didn't want to sleep around. I didn't want a broken home like the one I grew up in. I knew I wanted a family and kids from a very young age. It didn't take long for that relationship to become very violent. I was still a little meaty at the start of this relationship, but then I became tiny at forty-nine kilograms. I'm only five foot three inches, and my partner ended up getting very jealous of any attention I was getting and would take his anger out on me. I remember going out with my friends, who dropped me off the next morning in my PJs. I was feeling carefree until he took me into the bedroom, grabbed my g-string, and ripped it up my vagina like I'd done something wrong.

One day, I got my hair done for my friend's wedding. Feeling excited and beautiful as a lady should, I was so excited to see him. He came down from Sydney, as I was in Bomaderry at the time. He started a fight with me because I was in a classy dress for a wedding! This was an ongoing situation for any time we were heading out!

A RED FLAG ISN'T A RED FLAG WHEN IT FEELS LIKE HOME.

I guess I mistakenly clung onto someone loving me, after being fat and alone for so long. The first man who gave me attention and he reminded me of David Beckham! The yelling and the violence were what I knew. I'd grown up in a verbally abusive household, so the noise was familiar. I thought that's what love was.

Our relationship wasn't all bad. We did enjoy the beach, and we would spend holidays in Byron Bay. Summers were spent with as much time at the beach as we could. It was an on and off again relationship, once again mirroring the relationships I'd witnessed during my childhood. I ended that relationship when I grew stronger, realising that there was more to my life than ongoing abuse and being yelled at.

I moved to the Gold Coast when I was twenty-four, as it was a dream my best friend and I shared. I moved back to Bondi when I was twenty-nine, just in time to meet 'Mr Incredible'. Ha-ha. Ferds!

The Path that Led Me to the Cover

My best friend and I spoke of the Gold Coast at school and well yeah, we made our dreams a reality. I was living my best life! They were great days with parties and lots of drinking, but I still loved group fitness. Over time, I put a little weight back on from eating unhealthy food and drinking alcohol.

I decided feeling hung over wasn't what I wanted in my life, so I started focusing on my gym and food more as my mindset and health was starting to fail. I was tired, fatigued, and eating too much while watching Bridesmaids on a Sunday with a bowl of ice cream. My head was a wreck!

I loved group fitness so much that I decided to do my training for it, then became a fitness instructor. Becoming a good RPM instructor was hard for me, as I went straight into the entertainment side of giving the class, and my little legs couldn't hit a beat! I failed my first attempt at instructing, as I didn't understand how to pull back with my energy and teach a basic set up. I nearly gave up, but you know how it works. We don't give up. I got back on that bike and worked hard. I needed to step up with all my magic energy and learn to communicate more effectively, and I learned to use silence as a tool. How magical is silence! I love learning in silence and feeling the participants' energy when we ride quietly, knowing that we can work using our internal emotion.

Learning to understand and use the power of silence has been one of my biggest blessings. You can hear, listen, and learn so much in silence if you genuinely tap into your higher self. I became a very strong and incredible RPM instructor. The other programs I teach are my fun, but I tend to get over silly teaching body pump because it's not my strength, and my mind can wander a little. Ha-ha. Whoops!

I can't emphasise enough how important it is to never give up on your hopes and desires. No matter how many times you fail, don't give up on yourself and go after your goals.

So, what is it I do as my training? Well, are you ready for it? Ha-ha. BODYPUMP! Les Mills.

Again, most people say I'm obsessed with the gym, but the truth is I'm petrified of the place. I never step foot on the gym floor because of how I felt being fat when I started at seventeen. I still walk straight to the group fitness studio. If I'm not teaching group fitness, I'm doing it at 8am by myself. That's after I've done my morning routine of walking along the beach while the moon goes down and the sun comes up. I pump every day, and this is my routine seven days a week. I will take time to recover if my body needs it!

 SING IT - *PRISONER OF SOCIETY* - THE LIVING END

Chapter Eleven: Never Judge Unless You've Walked Someone's Path

notes

Chapter Twelve

health

Health to me is just my life. I don't view it as I did a run today so I can tick that box, or I ate well today so I can tick that box. I do what I do because I love it! I look forward to every day I live. I don't go out and party as it gives me anxiety, and it's not how I want to live my life.

After I do my walk or pump, I dive into the ocean. Yes, in winter and yes, in the rain. It awakens me. I genuinely feel like a new human and it's like my life has started at thirty-six. I'm free, happy, and healthy.

What are the benefits of cold-water therapy?

It fires up your lymphatic system.

It helps blood flow and circulation.

It helps with chronic fatigue.

It helps burn brown fat cells.

It helps with inflammation.

It helps with stress.

It makes your skin glow!

You get this amazing freedom, feeling like you're 18.

If you don't have an ocean near you, you can always finish your shower off with a cold-water blast. Once you get used to this, you'll be amazed at the benefits you will feel.

The Little Fat Kid in the Cupboard

AGE 17 to 23

DEAR DIARY,

I started my weight loss journey today. I'm just going to copy a model's diet from a magazine.

Today I ate:

* A bowl of Muesli. I'm loving this. I'm using skim milk. My favourite part is the sultanas, nuts, and bits of apricot.

* A salad wrap for lunch.

* For dinner, I had salmon with some spinach.

I am feeling great. I am running every morning and afternoon. However, I am also weighing myself every day. I'm being a little obsessive.

Today, I ran my ass off. I weighed myself at 49kg. I'm so excited to go out on Thursday, Friday, and Saturday night this week.

Today, I am hungover and haven't eaten much, but I did wake up and do body combat then go for a run so I can start drinking again this afternoon.

THE RESULT

My insides were unhealthy. I always had inflammation around my belly holding a lot of cortisol, and always had a pot belly. I was young. I was skinny/fat.

AGE 23 to 25

DEAR DIARY,

I moved to the Gold Coast and had the best night out. I stopped at the gelato shop on my way home. I scabbed some random person's money to get an extra scoop of Snickers. Ha-ha to that person, I thank you! Ha-ha.

THE RESULT

The effects of being hungover on a Sunday wasn't helping me move forward with my fitness goals. As being hungover stopped me from training, I ate my weight on a Sunday, and the week after made me lethargic.

AGE 25 to 27

DEAR DIARY,

I want to let go of the drinking life, as I've put weight back on. I'm sitting around 62kg. I am becoming obsessed with the scales, as I'm not back down to 49kg.

DEAR DIARY,

Today I feel fatigued and sluggish. I want my little pot belly to go. So, I got myself a coach who gave me a meal plan as I asked for a little guidance. He did tell me I might have food allergies or maybe I'm getting 'OLD', as I'm finding it hard to shift weight. How rude!

DEAR DIARY,

Today, I ate oats for breakfast with protein powder, and rice cakes and tuna for a snack.

Lunch was canned tuna with 12 almonds and the biggest bowl of vegetables because I was hungry, and I wanted to be full.

Dinner was chicken and vegetables.

I'm feeling really good.

DEAR DIARY,

Today I'm going to try 3 snakes (LOLLIES), as my coach said I can have 3 snakes or 3 pieces of fruit before participating in RPM.

TRIGGER!!! I became addicted to lollies. I couldn't stop myself from walking down the lolly aisle, pretending that I couldn't see them. I told myself that I was fine and strong and that I could resist the urge to buy them. But there I was grabbing a 300g bag of no name lollies. The bigger the bag, the better.

DEAR DIARY,

I am eating in my car so no one can see me. To the girl who hides in the car and eats, I see you, I feel you. You can get through this.

THE RESULT

I was becoming addicted to lollies. The sugar was like a cocaine high! The come down was not great. I was agitated and angry. I had sugar cravings that were winning daily. I had to stop myself from buying bags of lollies. And yet still I would walk down the lolly isle like an addict. I was addicted to the rush that the sugar in these lollies gave me.

My inner child wanted to escape. The sugar triggers us the way drugs do, and I craved a sugar hit. It has the same effect as alcohol. Emotionally, mentally, and physically, the ups and downs gave me chronic fatigue. I was in a very angry headspace. I noticed I was short tempered and snappy.

DEAR DIARY,

Today I am feeling sluggish, and still have a pot belly that is inflamed.

I went to the doctors to see if it was maybe hormonal. The doctor put me on 'DEPRESSION PILLS'.

Something is not right. I'm not a depressed person. He changed my contraceptive pill as he said it may be my hormones. Not once was food mentioned!

We all trust doctors, yet they don't have a certificate in nutrition. This is what most people can't get their head around. Why would a doctor hand me out drugs and not fix the main cause? Because it's bad for business. Very little time is spent on nutrition in their training.

We have been programmed to believe doctors and the media without even looking into the underlying course. For example, an ad comes on about Nutri-grain and we believe it's good for us. It's full of sugar and preservatives, and yet no one questions 'an expert' making millions. We are dumbed down and brainwashed.

Youtube: Cereal Makers Sold Us a Breakfast Myth
https://www.youtube.com/watch?v=9Ffceu672c4

THE RESULT

I was so sick and inflamed on the inside that I was becoming lost with who I was. I took myself off both the pills. I got a little angry for a while as I was coming off them, but felt so much better after a week. Physically, I was still fit.

DEAR DIARY,

Today, I am so skinny and feeling great, but I'm TIRED and fatigued! I can't move. I have given myself chronic fatigue. Who will ever want to date Ms. Farty butt? I have been so gassy.

I've been eating just vegetables. How are my insides so inflamed and sick from vegetables? They have defensive chemicals that are making us bloated and sick.

AGE 28 to 34

DEAR DIARY,

Today, I am teaching four classes. Giving Sydney a go. It's very fast and I'm finding I am getting very anxious with the crowds in the city. I can't keep up with my own feet. I am flat out busy.

Today, I ate oats for breakfast, and I bought a massive salad with chicken and avocado to help get me through my afternoon classes. I am just drained emotionally, physically, and mentally. Dad being sick with cancer isn't helping me right now. I'm trying to be kind to my heart.

DEAR DIARY,

Today, I ate a small bowl of oats. I'll have chicken and salad for lunch. Then for dinner, I'll have the biggest BOX ha-ha vegetables to get me through my night. I probably overate. I'm very bloated, but I've let go of the scales and I genuinely am happy with how I feel. I don't care what the number is anymore.

I never weigh myself. I got rid of them at 30 years old. They only upset me, and I feel amazing in my clothes, so there is no point worrying about what you weigh. If the scales affect you and make you feel down, don't do it! Just concentrate on how you feel with what you wear.

DEAR DIARY,

Now I'm dating a man. I should not eat so many vegetables because they make me bloated and gassy. I'll eat my oats, chicken salad, and fruit. I'm feeling really good. I can't have pears though. I get embarrassed by fluffing. It's not very cute. I love pears, but they affect me.

AGE 35 to 36 and a 1/2

DEAR DIARY,

I am struggling with my emotions, as I'm feeling like my soul and life has been sucked out of me after the breakup with Mr Perfect himself. My eating habits have been really good. I just need some guidance at this time in my life.

I found 'THE NATURAL TRANSFORMER', Joel Bushby. He is incredible and to anyone who needs a little hand, I recommend him. He helped me believe in myself and helped me during a time I needed someone's hand to hold.

If the scales affect you and make you feel down, don't do it!

Just concentrate on how you feel with what you wear.

DEAR DIARY,

Today I ate my five meals:

Oats for breakfast with protein powder.

Then rice cakes with tuna at 11:00 am.

I had a chicken salad with a ¼ cup rice.

I had a protein shake for afternoon tea with some yogurt and five almonds, then chicken salad for dinner. I am feeling great.

DEAR DIARY,

Finally, I am so happy. It's been two weeks on my food plan, and I'm allowed my 'CHEAT/TREAT'. I ate Weet-Bix with salted caramel protein powder. OMG! I think this is what heaven feels like. I'll just have a few more. Um okay, I have no milk left. I've had half a box of Weetbix and all the milk. 'Are you for real Bruce? 'How many can you do?'

DEAR DIARY,

The 5 nuts I'm allowed turned to 25 and again, I found myself overeating. I was triggered. I'm not very good at this snack or portion thing people talk about.

In saying that, I've always been fit on the outside. I've always been positive and a very happy girl. I've always understood how important health is, and I have a deep desire and will to always move forward in my personal growth, and understanding myself, my body, and fitness. It is so important to be open and willing to explore and learn new things about oneself and life.

THE RESULT

I kept noticing the same patterns with my eating. I loved the volume, and these carbohydrates were triggers to my past. I remember eating Weet-Bix for dinner like a kid, with extra brown sugar. YUM. However, they were making me feel tired.

DEAR DIARY,

I can't be trusted with food in my cupboard, like when I was a little girl. I just want to sit in it to feel safe and comfortable, eating Milo without milk. Ha-ha.

I found myself at 37

DEAR DIARY,

I've been doing some research with the carnivore diet. I think I'm going to give it a go. I'm at a steady place with my body, and I'd like to see what the fuss is all about. I mean nothing has worked for me so far, and I want to see if it's what I'm needing. Who doesn't love steak?!

DEAR DIARY,

Today is day 8 on the carnivore diet. I'm feeling incredible. My bloating has disappeared, and my energy is much higher. I've noticed I'm not craving food or looking at the cupboard to find some food, even though I'm in a van and I don't have one. Ha-ha.

DEAR DIARY,

Today is week two into the carnivore diet and still going strong. Love, love, loving it. I'm a new person today. I had steak for meal one, chicken for meal two, then I had some papaya around 3 pm. I have no crash, no cravings, and I'm noticing I've cured my chronic fatigue and any inflammation I've given myself from my past eating habits.

DEAR DIARY,

Today marks my 3 months of being a carnivore. I have really noticed my life on every level has just changed. I'm so happy. I have no depressed thoughts. I'm living in each moment.

Today I am trying just two bigger meat meals - a massive steak for meal one, and some lamb for meal two so I'll be fasting from 2 pm until 8 am.

DEAR DIARY,

5 months into carnivore and I've definitely let go of the fruit. Trying to just stick with fruit every 4th or 5th day. Two big meals are what works best for me. Feeling so lean and happy.

DEAR DIARY,

Today, someone told me I look happier than ever. My aura is shining and it's beautiful. I genuinely believe the carnivore diet has saved my life. I am living the highest life I can. I have no inflammation or cortisol in my body.

THE RESULT

I've healed my insides. I'm living a higher, happier life. What carbs are you speaking of? Ha-ha.

How do you start?

We are all different and we all want different goals. We can't all eat the same thing to achieve a personal goal. My goals are to stay small and lean, to be able to stay fit and healthy, and to move my body for the rest of my life with a happy, clear mind, free from negative thoughts.

I guess with weight loss, you need to think of it like this - calories in versus calories out. If you want to lose weight, you need to be in a calorie deficit.

What is that?

It means that you put less food in your mouth than the calories you burn in a day, so move more and eat less. It's that simple.

I'm not one to weigh my food either. That adds stress and cortisol for me. However; weighing portions might work best for you.

De stress, Eat Less

We want to stay away from cortisol. What is cortisol? It's a stress hormone in our bodies that holds on to fats around our core. Cortisol is activated when the body is stressed (i.e.from certain foods that cause inflammation,not enough sleep, unhealthy choices in life, and overtraining or overworking your body). You will hold onto cortisol in your abdomen area, and can put on a lot of weight.

Our aim is to bring our cortisol down. Changing your diet can lower your cortisol. Food from the shelf does an amazing job of feeding your body stress by adding numbers (toxins in the form of flavouring, preservatives, and colours) into your body. You are telling your brain, 'You don't give a fuck so make me feel like SHIT!'

An example of me raising my cortisol is when I teach too many classes in a week. My cortisol goes up and I put weight on. I say it's so much fun, but my body says, oh no, it's not! Ha-ha. You can train and keep cortisol levels low by walking, and doing weights or low impact exercise. That's the beauty of it - just move!

And sleep - if I don't get my 9/10 hours of sleep, I am not okay. My cortisol rises, and I get in a very upset head space. Sleep is so important for recovery, growing, healing, weight loss, and mental health.

YOU'RE THE PRODUCT. THEY DON'T CARE IF YOU ARE SICK. THEY ARE RICH!

Have you looked at what the numbers stand for?

The seed oil that is in most of your food? Chemicals that give US CANCER.

That is what is killing us, changing our hormones, and making children sick.

Foods can change your hormones and microbiome. Why is transgender on the rise? I bet the kids eat preservatives. They don't have any healthy food in their diet. They are so lost with who they are due to addictions, fast food, technology, and social media just to name a few. Is it any wonder they are feeling lost and depressed?

Who gets the money? Big pharma.

Who creates everyone being sick? The same big companies and corporations.

Who sits back with their millions? Bill Gates?

AND FUCKING IDIOTS BELIEVE THEY CARE? Who announces them saving you? The media.

The brands are so smart at keeping kids addicted. They know what they are doing. You are the product. They use you to make their millions of dollars. Most people don't look at the numbers and the fillers and what they are. They trust a company with a tick!

Sugar is a drug like ice - just wondering if you'd feed your kid ice? Sugar is having the same effect mentally and emotionally, and now with depression and anxiety on the rise, we wonder why it's happening. Then, cancer and mental illness comes in after years of using drugs.

I was manic sometimes as a kid because I lived off cereal, and gave myself a good start of failure.

Once, I ate a whole packet of chewing gum when I was working in the city. Why? Because I had it on me. Ha-ha. However, the next day I woke up feeling like I'd been on drugs! My point is, even sugar free stuff is not good for us. In fact, it's worse. We need to think about all the chemicals identified as numbers on packaging that we put into our bodies. It is poison. It changes the hormones in us as individuals.

When I consume preservatives and chemicals contained in food, my head gets very agitated, and it upsets me. I can get very snappy.

My Gut Told Me!
NO ONE TALKS ABOUT HEALTH!

Doctors have a degree to hand out pills that lower our immunity. Take a pill if you are depressed. They treat the symptom and not the cause. We are not our diagnosis! What we need to understand is that our food goes to our gut first. Our gut is our second brain, and it's more powerful than our brain. Food doesn't land in your brain; your gut spreads the word. If we look at people who are overweight with swelling and scabs on their feet, it's because their GUT is so damaged and inflamed with all the shit food they are eating, It's killing their insides and life. Then the gut says to the brain, 'Well, you know what mate? I am unable to help control your walking anymore because you have been sending me really shit signals.' It is all connected.

Let's look at a few foods that might upset you without knowing it. It can be something as simple as yogurt, bread, gluten, or milk. I don't eat any of these foods, nor do I have any carbohydrates apart from fruit. I know because my face swells up from eating dairy. My eyes swell up from rice cakes. You can start removing certain foods to remove brain fog. Try to start with something like bread, then remove more as you feel better. Think baby steps. When you start eating foods that your body can use and avoid the ones causing problems, you won't believe how much better you feel. It's like a lightbulb moment or diving in the ocean. It gives you that spring in your step. That's why I move and act like I'm twenty-five, and that's what I want for me for the rest of my life.

Try the carnivore elimination diet if you want to get the best results - just meat, water, and salt.

For a few weeks then, you can have a play around with adding fruit if it's not sitting right for you.

The Four People Diet Types
'Is that mine?' the FAT HEART girl said to the SNACK KID.

The SNACK KID said, 'I have two cupcakes. You can have one, I'm full'.

The FAT HEART girl was so happy. Her heart filled up with so much joy.

Then, along came the kid who had a full lunch box called THE SHARE BEAR. The

Chapter Twelve: Health

FAT HEART was just staring into the full lunch box, hoping she could eat her food. The SHARE BEAR. gave the girl her sandwich because she wasn't hungry, and the FAT HEART was so happy. The SNACK KID didn't budge, and the SHARE BEAR got in trouble for handing out her food.

Then, how can we forget the HEALTHY KID with carrot sticks? It's always carrot sticks, apples, a yoghurt, and half a salad wrap. No junk! Well, THE FAT HEART, SNACK KID, and SHARE BEAR all stared at her food. Let's call them THE SILVER SPOON!

I guess this silly little story is how you work out where you sit with your eating. It really depends on what kind of kid you are and where you start.

So, I'll break it down with four simple ways to start a diet. Think about what kid you are, then you can work out what is the best way for YOU!

THE FAT HEART KID - I'm with you. We just don't feel full. Basically, you are in or you're out. I tend to always want a big meal. A piece of fruit will not do it for me, and I can be a bottomless pit, meaning that I find it better to not eat at all rather than having something small, otherwise I will keep on eating. My suggestion would be that you could just do 500g of steak as a first meal, or if you don't want to be carnivore, you can have a protein shake with avocado or banana. You can have two meals as meal one and then eat once a day. Add fruit when you are hungry, and try to stay away from foods with preservatives. I'd consider fasting for you to close the window of eating.

THE SNACK KID - You seem to be able to survive on small snacks, and I'm definitely jealous of you. Ha-ha. I have written a few perfect meals for you and your health. Again, it depends whether you want to try carnivore or not. You can start with a small steak, then you could do some avocado or some fruit as a snack. This is how I started, or you can do what my sister is trying. She's having a steak and chicken at 2 pm, then she loves her oats, so has them with protein powder at 5 pm. as her second and last meal. She has oats daily, so she knows she can have a treat. It keeps her on track and still in a calorie deficit.

THE SHARE BEAR - How we love you! You're probably not hungry, and now it's 2 pm and you're thinking to yourself, 'Shit, I need food!' You are in the best position to do a bigger portion so you're full, or you can split meals into two. I suggest you reach for a higher fat meal with avocado, or even some salmon if you're struggling to have a decent meal. Or if you don't want to be carnivore, try eggs and avocado, probably with the coffee you forgot to drink. Ha-ha.

SILVER SPOON - How blessed you are to have a steady healthy diet from a young age with structure. You probably get bored and need lots of different foods on rotation, or love a good recipe. Ha-ha. I hate following recipes but if you do like them, that's fine, just stay away from seed oils, corn (no good), and double check what ingredients you really are using. Make sure they are all clear from numbers, as numbers on food can change your microbiome. Try to stay away from grains.

It's what works for you. This is why a 'DIET' doesn't work for so many people. Imagine having an eating disorder, then being forced to just have one cupcake. It's like telling a recovering ice addict to just try a line of coke.

Don't Booty Call Me

I go to bed with the moon and rise with the sun. Sleep is most important when it comes to health. I do enjoy a good nine to ten hours of sleep a night with no blue light when heading to bed. Then, I open my eyes to the sunlight in the morning while I'm walking.

I'm a massive believer that the blue light on our iPads, phones, and computers are affecting our health and minds. I know because when it rains for a week and I'm on my phone more, I get headaches, and feel drained and very unbalanced with extra anxiety. We don't belong on our phones. Not to mention what the radiation (EMFs) are doing to us, please use flight mode at night, or better still, turn everything off.

I have always needed sleep, and I genuinely believe my circadian rhythm is on point. I'm so connected to the moon and sunlight, and I feel this has been one of my biggest blessings with my health, helping me keep focused and on track.

I really appreciate my state swimming days for giving me structure in my life, and my mummy who had to drive me to the pool regularly at 5 am.

I get all my vitamin D from the sun daily. It's our highest energy source, yet it's said to be the bad guy who's giving us cancer. It's the toxins in the oils most people use like CANOLA OIL that's the culprit. This is a perfect example of poison! Have you looked at what is in this? It's evil.

We need to be outside more, as people are becoming sick mentally from no sun. It's pure medicine! After my spiritual awakening, I'm now noticing that we should do everything opposite to what the ads and media say.

Fasting

An early dinner gives us a better fasting window. Our body needs to fast. I sleep better, and I know my body is healing and recovering while I sleep ready for the next day. The one thing I've learnt in my years of health and fitness is the less I eat in the afternoon, the better and clearer my mind is when I wake up. I have extra energy as my body is in deep sleep, and not focusing on digesting my food.

I fast for 16 hours most days. I try to have my last meal by 2 pm. I've only brought this in since I've become a carnivore. You can fast and not eat breakfast if that works for you - perfect. Therefore, I call it meal one, meal two or meal three rather than labelling them as they have been traditionally. Have your first meal at 12 pm. We don't need to set a rule. My sister eats her first meal at 1 pm. and the last meal by 7:30 pm. This is what works for her, but it wouldn't work for me.

Meats I love are salmon, barramundi, steak, lamb, and chicken. If you can afford it, buy organic, support our farmers, and rock on!

My favourite fruits are banana, watermelon, mango, and papaya. I love dates, but they are very high in sugar, so I try not to buy them. They give me inflammation and an insulin spike. They remind me of sticky date pudding from when I was a kid. Ha-ha-ha.

I get asked this question a lot. Do you eat meat for breakfast? I ask, do you eat cereal because that's a rule and that's all you know? How's your brain fog going for you? How's the energy you have? How's your fatigue and inflammation? I say, really ask yourself if you think you are healthy and on fire with life. Are you excited about life? Maybe you need to try the carnivore diet. You can go full speed meat, or just start charging your meal one for now.

My head is clear, and I don't crash in the afternoons. I find I can focus more. My moods are steady. When my periods are due. My stabbing pain and fatigue are so much better. In fact, I used to get so crampy, and I would be in so much pain. but now I don't experience this so much anymore as my inside isn't inflamed and it's not tripled with swelling once a month. Ha-ha.

Are you Craving Carbs?

Think of this: when you crave carbs, sugars, or chocolate, It's because that's all your mind knows. If you eat carbohydrates or sugar for breakfast, you are feeding your second brain, which is your gut. This sends messages to your brain throughout the day, so that you will crave more sugars or carbohydrates. So, if you get hungry, carbs and sugars are the foods that you will reach for.

You need to flip this on its head and eat a protein,fat, or both for breakfast to tell your second brain - your gut - that you will be full and all you need to eat is more protein and fat throughout the day, not carbs and sugars. You will start to

reprogram your brain to reach for protein and fat for an energy source, and this will also help with inflammation and disease. As a population, we are the sickest and the saddest that we have ever been, yet I'm the happiest I've ever been.

Due to being carnivore, I don't crave the toxins that are now in many processed and supermarket foods. People don't realise how addictive these foods are. Generally, we are eating less red meat but eating more pills, because no one can 'BE BOTHERED' to cure themselves and a pill or a quick fix just puts a Band-Aid on over the issue. This shuts down your immunity. We want to build our immunity. Why is this happening? Because we are programmed to believe the TV and the media. Turn it off and think about it.

If you don't eat meat, that's fine. Boil some eggs, have some avocado, or find a good protein powder that sits well on your gut. I stick to THE NATURAL TRANSFORMERS. They are all natural products that don't upset my stomach.

Keep it simple.

DEAR DIARY,

Today, I said my prayers to the Heavenly Father and the cow I ate as he gave me a better life. I am getting better at saying my prayers towards animals, as I really appreciate how I feel. I love cows and I hope they live a great life. My life is important and I'm so grateful. I feel my vibration of living has shifted to new heights.

Yours sincerely,

Fat Heart
oxoxo

THE RESULT

I have a higher quality of life, and I feel I am thriving every morning when I wake up. 'CARNIVORE MD' is a man I look up to, and get a lot of my information from.

Alcohol

Consuming alcohol always leads to a massive conversation about fitness and health. None of those words go together. There is not one part of alcohol, fitness, and health that match, I'm sorry to say. Ha-ha.

I gave up drinking at 28 as it's not my thing. I don't enjoy it and it doesn't give me the results I want. If you drink and you are complaining about your health or weight, cutting alcohol would be a great help.

You can stick to vodka, lime, and soda as the less calorie option, however it's the next day when you crave and eat all the extra food you think you want when the damage is done. It won't level itself out in calories. You'll end up eating twice as many calories hungover as what you would normally, so I'll leave that one with you. Also, when you drink alcohol and you've got to train, you are only burning off the alcohol, not the food or your body fat. This is another setback.

If you want to start to change, think baby steps, so you don't go in full speed and become hard on yourself. You know the old 'I'll start Monday?' Well, most of the time, people fail after six weeks. I genuinely believe it is because people go full speed into their new way of eating, and it sets them up to fail because they can't maintain what it takes to achieve the extreme goal that they've set for themselves when they walk into the gym. The thing with fitness is it doesn't just happen, and results may take longer than six weeks to show. I'm constantly working on my goals. It's my life! I don't see it as a challenge, so start with soft baby steps and start small.

A perfect example of taking small steps is as follows. Set your weekly intention. For example, this week I will do an hour walk every day and eat a protein breakfast. That will be a massive achievement. Then, add an extra intention the following week. After the two weeks, you can look back at how far you've come.

How will you transform your mind, soul, health, and most of all, YOUR STORY? People often say, 'I can't because I'm old or fat.' That's you telling yourself a story. Change it to a positive mindset. Say 'I can, and I will'. We are becoming so negative about ourselves. I'm nearly forty, but I feel like I am eighteen. You can change.

Your Mindset Changes You

I was working on a chocolate spin wheel once as a promotion girl. It had $100 and free parking as one of the prizes. Me being annoyingly observant, I just watched and listened to people. Sixty percent of the people who came up said, 'I won't win. I will never win.' Their shoulders slumped, with their energy and negative mindset pulling them down, down. Well, you know what? They got free parking, then I said, 'See. I told you.' Again, I didn't say anything, except congratulations. Ha-ha. However, this beautiful guy came sparkling along and said, 'I'm manifesting the $100.' His energy was beautiful, and I felt his hand saying 'Hand me the $100!' as he bought some tickets. I stood there just knowing he was going to win. Then, boom! We looked at each other with this magical look. YES, QUEEN! He'd won the $100. It's all about the mindset. Flip the bad thoughts on their head. Be positive. Believe you can.

Meditating on JOE DISPENZA has honestly changed my mind set. Start practicing talking to yourself only using positive words and start pulling in your future. You are the creator.

I guess what I've learnt in my life is that no one is coming to help me. No one is going to do it for you, and no one is going to take those first few steps for you. It is a hard truth, I know, but it's a fact. You do what is needed for you, but you need to do the hard work, and by hard work I mean hard work. I'm writing and it's 3:30 am. No one sees the hard work that anyone puts in. You know when people tell you how lucky you are to have a house or a nice body? Well, I say, 'Funny that. The harder I work, the luckier I seem to get.' Ha-ha. It's all in you and your mind set. Once you change your mindset, you change your world!

Today is your new day, and each day is a chance for a new beginning or a fresh start, even if you didn't get where you wanted the day before.

You can start small. What would my baby step suggestion be? WALK. Go on beach walks or bush walks or walk around your neighbourhood. Do an hour walk daily on an empty stomach, or with that black coffee. This will be a massive achievement, and it's one of the best ways to burn fat and keep that cortisol away.

From my heart to yours. I've created your first motivational playlist to move to. The songs I've written at the end of each chapter have all had a special place in my heart, whether I've cried, danced, yelled, or trained my ass off to them. Some might be my favourite Les Mills songs. I feel they create an amazing playlist for you, so you can remember you can do whatever your mind says it will do.

Enjoy walking, running, or singing. For inspiration, you'll have me with you all the way annoyingly singing. I'm proud of you!

SING IT - *GLITTER* **- PINK**

SING IT - *THIS IS ME* **- THE GREATEST SHOWMAN**

Chapter Twelve: Health

notes

Chapter Thirteen
pink rock

You have more power, so be true to yourself. They have no place in your heart and no place in your energy field, so give them nothing.

Chapter Thirteen: Pink Rock

You've heard me speak about the Pink Rock in my story, but what on earth am I on about?

The pink rock is a symbol to aim for. For me, it symbolises healing, strength, and forgiveness towards myself, and letting go of pain and anger to move forward with my healthier inner self.

The Grey Rock is a phrase used in psychology. The meaning behind it is about closing the door to a narcissist. By closing the door, I mean blocking them completely out of your life. Imagine the grey rock is a straight out, solid force, door slam block. Go cold turkey with the abusive narcissist or ex-partner. Get rid of them, and move upward. The grey rock is used to protect someone from further hurt.

And why? For a narcissist to keep their supply, they'll keep a supply of any kind available, and won't ever close the door or give you closure. They get off on hurting you or even just seeing you. Their minds think you want them back and they always want the upper hand of control. They genuinely get off on seeing what you are doing and thinking, especially if they see you confused and in emotional pain. They can hoover you back, as it's all about the power and control they have over you. This is where you need to use the Grey Rock. Slam those doors shut on this type of person and regain control of your life.

So why is the grey rock so powerful? YOU take your life and control back.

Most people ask how they can get back at their narcissist ex. This is your answer: They don't want you to succeed without them. SO, LEVEL UP! They hate it. They want you to need them. The thing with a narcissist is that they need to be the instigator, and love any kind of reaction or emotional response. Why? Any kind of reaction from you towards them is heaven to them, because they know they can still trigger you. So, act like they are a puff of smoke. If you see them or they message you, give them nothing. Whatever you do, give them no energy on any level.

A narcissist hates it if you do not notice or acknowledge them. Why? They hate losing control, and hate thinking you have your power and worth back. The grey rock is slamming the door blocking them.

I like to say PINK ROCK. Imagine the Pink Rock is like giving a gift to yourself. You walk away with more grace and elegance. It's about giving back to you. You have more power, so be true to yourself. They have no place in your heart and no place in your energy field, so give them nothing.

Remember, you are too beautiful and wonderful to let someone take your magical soul away. Hold that beautiful heart of yours for the people in your life who deserve your love. Know you are loved, and that you are beautiful and strong.

It's also about letting go and forgiving yourself. Forgive yourself for being attracted to a narcissist or for being in a bad relationship. Forgiving and forgetting is the process that you must go through as part of your healing process. Remember that forgiving someone doesn't mean you excuse them for what they did to you; it means that you are no longer willing to carry around the pain that they caused you. Once you have done the work, you are well on your way to healing, but we always need to practise a strong mind set and bring in our new future.

It's time to move forward and level up in your life. PINK ROCK! Be the sparkling light you are.

Chapter Thirteen: Pink Rock

notes

Chapter Fourteen

my purpose and my vision

To find your purpose, ask: What makes you happy? What makes your heart smile? For me, it's the beach, freedom, love, simplicity, beach walks, being outside, not being on my phone, exercising, writing, helping others, and group fitness. I can live my best life and feel complete by incorporating all the above into my days. What story are you going to stop telling yourself so you can find your purpose? What are you doing that is sabotaging your goals?

My vision is to close this book and hand on my heart say, 'I have told my story to hopefully awaken someone.'

I want to show you that you can come back from rock bottom and become stronger than you were yesterday. Every day is a new day, so high five yourself for reading this book and for taking that step outside of your comfort zone to walk into your new future that you have manifested. If it was a challenge, and you took that baby step towards what you want and what you deserve, be a little prouder. I am proud of you! Be proud of yourself too.

To help my beautiful empaths, understand we have superpowers. We are super brains, and we will always help others. Remember putting yourself first is your biggest strength, with baby steps you can - and you will - make yourself your number one priority. You can do anything with extra boundaries and following your intuition. We know and understand the difference between KIND and NICE.

To level up, chase your dream, and speak to the Heavenly Father/Universe to get your answers. Jump more and take more control in your life. Level up, follow your intuition, and trust it.

CHASE YOUR DREAM.

Here is your last FUCK! PINK ROCK!

 SING IT - *AFFIRMATION* - SAVAGE GARDEN

Why the Pretty Pictures?

When I was sixteen, I would look outside my window, crying and dreaming of being the pretty girl you see on the cover of a magazine. I prayed from a young age. I DID IT. I've always had a connection with my spirit. I dreamt, I spoke, and I always got my answers. I believed the golden mask was inside me all along.

 SING IT - *UNWRITTEN* - NATASHA BEDINGFIELD

notes

the people I need to thank

Jamie Ryder - Coach (Who I now call a friend)

Jeremy Mansueto - Photographer

Cherine Waddell - Makeup Artist

Stacey Davidson - Editor

Mos the Label - Dresses

Paul Saladino - Carnivore MD

Nutrition with Judy - The Carnivore Elimination Diet

Judy Cho and Laura Spath - Cutting Against the Grain

Lewis Howes - School of Greatness

Joe Dispenza - Walking into Your Future

Ally Mosher - Graphic Designer

one year later ...

I've built all my resilience.

I'm a warrior.

Living in my van for now, floating free.

The Cookie Monster is his name.

I've moved back to the Gold Coast.

I wake to the moon, the sun, the beach, and my beautiful fairy lights.

I now have a very healthy work life balance.

Selling my book.

I'm now 100% carnivore.

My mind is clear.

My energy is high.

And I've written a kids book called *"I woke up so mad today"*.

How did I get to this magical moment where I am now?

By believing in myself,

asking the heavenly father for guidance,

being unapologetically me,

following my intuition when I tapped into my heart.

Follow the Rainbow!

www.ingramcontent.com/pod-product-compliance
Lightning Source LLC
Chambersburg PA
CBHW081709100526
44590CB00022B/3709